ROBERT L. PERRY

FIND A NICHE

and Scratch It

Marketing Your
Congregation

Foreword by Robert D. Dale

The Alban Institute

Library of Congress Catalog Number 2002116296

ISBN 1-56699-275-3

To the three outstanding church associations that I have been privileged to serve:

Clay-Platte Baptist Association, Liberty, Missouri (1984–1988)

Mount Vernon Baptist Association, Annandale, Virginia (1988–1997)

Richmond Baptist Association, Richmond, Virginia (1997–Present)

In most faith traditions, the district association or regional grouping of congregations is the oldest level of inter-church cooperation and missions endeavor. Each of the associations I have served afforded me the opportunity to fulfill my calling, great freedom to be true to my gifts and personality, and constant challenge to learn and grow. The staff in all three associations were unusually skilled, dedicated, and effective. The church pastors, staff members, and laity were generally supportive, encouraging, and generous in their participation in the associations. Much of who I am and what I have learned has come from these associations of churches, so it is appropriate that this book be dedicated to them.

CONTENTS

FOREWORD

Unmet Need + Niche Focus = Successful Ministry

An unmet need is a motivator. Observers of human behavior have always recognized this simple fact. If you and I have personal or spiritual needs that remain unsatisfied, we will look for ways to meet those needs. Bob Perry has built on this foundational characteristic of individual and group life. This experienced consultant has mapped ways church leaders can identify unmet needs and then design ministries to meet those motivated needs.

Focusing ministry on niches of unmet needs can open fresh opportunities in your church for successful ministry. Are you and your church ready to discover niches of unmet needs? Your response to this simple question is important, because this equation, UN+NF=SM (Unmet Need plus Niche Focus equals Successful Ministry), has broad application. Consider these seven reasons for successful ministry:

1. Ministering to unmet needs is a basic biblical and theological theme.

Jesus' outreach to Zacchaeus in Luke 19 and to the woman at the well in John 4 are New Testament incidents of ministry to needs that still motivated those persons. In addition, Augustine's insight that persons have a God-shaped void that remains restless until we open our lives to God shows how hungry we are for God to meet all of our needs. Can you and your church build ministry on godly principles?

2. Ministering to unmet needs fits churches of all sizes.

Small churches sometimes feel they have no room for creativity in ministry and settle for too little. Larger churches sometimes try to be all things to all people and lose overall focus. Zeroing in on unmet needs both stretches and targets ministries for churches without regard to congregational membership size. Can you and your congregation find ministry opportunities in your area that will touch unreached groups of people without being biased by prejudgments based on the size of your church?

3. Ministering to unmet needs is a timeless strategy.
When unmet needs are the basic planning principle for ministry, both "the old, old story" of traditions and the latest trend in ministry can be considered and woven into a congregation's ministry future. Can you and your church plan for what Len Sweet calls its "AncientFuture" in ministry?

4. Ministering to unmet needs is portable.
Too many churches have forced their prospective members and their ministry and mission outreach prospects to "come here." When unmet needs are the focus of congregational efforts, ministry happens wherever needs and resources meet—sometimes in the neighborhoods and institutions of your community, sometimes within the walls of your church building. Can you and your church make ministry completely portable and flexible as you go there?

5. Ministering to unmet needs brims with balance.
Remember the diet God served the Hebrews in the wilderness? Manna—literally translated "What is it?"—was a balanced diet, providing both bread for the body and food for the soul. Niche ministry challenges us to serve both body and soul rather than focusing on one to the exclusion of the other. The Scripture describes the balance plainly: "He humbled you by letting you hunger, then by feeding you with manna, with which neither you nor your ancestors were acquainted, in order to make you understand that one does not live by bread alone, but by every word that comes from the mouth of the Lord" (Deut. 8:3). Can you and your church offer holistic outreach to whole persons?

6. Ministering to unmet needs is Christian stewardship.
The energy humans have to pursue their unmet needs is what psychologists call motivation. But, theologians describe this energy differently. We call it the Holy Spirit or God at work within us. Seen theologically, energy is never to be squandered. It is God's gift to us and to congregational life and is to

be channeled and used. It is our Christian stewardship. Can you and your church use ministry opportunities fully and well?

7. Ministering to unmet needs turns the spotlight toward others. Churches can become ingrown and self-absorbed. In fact, if you check your congregation's budget and programs, you will probably find that most of your resources and efforts are targeted on members of the congregation instead of on outsiders to the congregation. Servanthood calls Christians to reach out to others. Can you and your church keep others in the foreground of ministry?

Bob Perry has offered great advice: "Find a niche, and scratch it." Minister from your strengths to their needs, and your ministry will flourish. An unmet need is a motivator. Go for it!

BOB DALE
Director,
Center for Creative Church Leadership Development
Richmond, Virginia

ACKNOWLEDGMENTS

I want to acknowledge the assistance on this book from my insightful and capable wife, Dr. Marilyn C. Nelson. Marilyn assisted me with some of the consultation work involved in the book, and she carefully proofread every word I wrote, making important corrections and helpful suggestions.

I am grateful for consistent support from Jody Harlow, my administrative assistant at the Richmond Baptist Association, and for the rest of my team there.

Andrea S. L. Schieber and Beth Ann Gaede, my editors at the Alban Institute, were patient and encouraging in the process of refining this material and preparing it for publication. Their help in reworking the material, and their dedication to making the book understandable and user friendly, is responsible for significant improvements in it.

Pastor Michael Olmsted and the people of University Heights Baptist Church in Springfield, Missouri, were most gracious. They provided us with a caring church home during the summer of this writing, and they allowed us to use them as a pilot project for market-based planning.

Our other lab church was RiverSouth Community Church in Chesterfield County, Virginia. Their pastor, the Rev. Ty Cope, has been a good friend and a faithful encourager.

Dr. Robert Dale, director of the Center for Creative Church Leadership Development in Richmond, Virginia, has affirmed my writing efforts and his giftedness as a mentor has been empowering for me and for scores of others.

Beyond all other acknowledgments, I offer thanks and honor to the God whom I believe creates life, sustains life in this beautiful world, and makes life abundant through Jesus Christ.

Introduction

I have had the privilege of serving congregations and regional fellowships of congregations for the past 40 years. I have been a parish pastor, a foreign missionary, and the executive for several regional judicatories. In addition I have been honored to serve as a consultant in many of these same settings through the years. It has been a wonderful journey of learning and growth as I have attempted to better understand and more effectively lead these communities of faith.

In the course of my years of service to congregations, I spent seven years as a missionary serving churches in Mexico. What immediately became obvious as I began my work in Mexico was that I would have to learn a new language and develop an understanding of a new culture. It is precisely the absence of that sensitivity toward understanding the culture and speaking the language of the people among whom they live that stands in the way of effective ministry for many American congregations. During the decades of burgeoning congregational growth in the 1950s and '60s, we became comfortable living in a world where churched people were the majority, and where the popular culture valued a faith foundation. For many in our time it has become difficult to learn to relate in this foreign environment of a postmodern age. For some time I have felt that there was a need for a book that would help congregations better understand how to relate to the cultures and subcultures in which they were conducting their ministries.

This book deals in the area of congregational growth, but I do not use that term to refer only to numerical growth in the size of a congregation. We have, too often, defined success in congregational enterprise as increasing the numbers of noses and nickels. This is an inadequate

1

understanding of how and why congregations grow. The genuine healthy, growing congregation will reflect quality as well as quantity in its accomplishments.

This book is an effort to apply the principles and transferable learnings of the discipline of business marketing to the life and expansion of the communities of faith. I recognize that this application of secular and corporate marketing principles to the life of the congregation will cause some discomfort with some readers. Let me make it clear that I do not intend to abandon the principle of integrity in efforts at congregational development. No pragmatic use of secular methods should be pursued if it violates the basic theological, ethical, or ecclesiastical standards by which faith groups order their work. It is possible, however, to learn from the wisdom of secular disciplines and make application of that wisdom to congregational life. That translation can be done without doing damage to the integrity of the faith.

One of the helpful insights for me in thinking through this question of using corporate methods to achieve spiritual ends, was the realization that there are many instances in the Bible where people applied sound business practices and corporate leadership skills to their spiritual work. As I looked at the ministry of Jesus through this lens, I discovered that he was a very skilled practitioner of customer-sensitive marketing. Some people do a certain amount of market analysis intuitively and naturally. They seem to have an innate sense of who their customers are and how to reach them. Jesus seemed to be one of those natural niche marketers. He had no MBA, and he had not read the books on organizational leadership and marketing, but he was uniquely adept in the art of reading people. He fit his approach to the precise needs and interests of the person with whom he was dealing, and he spoke the cultural language of that individual. He not only had great sensitivity to the cultural context of the person, but he also understood his or her heart cry.

We need only look at some of the conversations Jesus had with people, as recorded in the New Testament, to see the depth of his insight into the human situation in general, and the specific life issues facing particular persons. No two conversations Jesus had with people are the same. He had no canned presentation, no pat answers to commonly raised objections, no rehearsed opening sentence or closing technique. He was never manipulative or coercive, but he was always attentive, respectful, and attuned to the person with whom he was speaking.

The Niche:
Wealthy and Young Influentials

In Luke 18:18 and following, we read about the encounter Jesus had with a young man who was described as a rich, young ruler. Each of these descriptive words is significant. "Rich" would indicate that he had lived a life of privilege and material prosperity. It implies that this may have been not only a fact about his life situation, but a point of pride and self-aggrandizement for him. He saw himself, and enjoyed having others see him, as a person of considerable material means.

"Young" is also a meaningful descriptor in this context. The man may have been in his twenties or even younger, perhaps a dozen years younger than Jesus. For many of us at that age, there was a great sense of our own immortality. I recall, now with some amusement, the risky and unwise behaviors in which I engaged during that period of my life. My hobbies included riding motorcycles, driving automobiles too fast, and quick-draw pistol shooting. (The pistol practice was only aimed at things that did not shoot back, but I still ran the risk of shooting my own toe.) The young man to whom Jesus was speaking was aware of and pleased with his youth. He was strong, healthy, and we can imagine, good looking. This was probably another point of personal pride for him.

To be described as a ruler in Jewish culture during that time was an indication of social, political, and probably religious influence. It may have meant a seat in the Sanhedrin or some other elite class of society. Again, the mention of these particular words of description would imply that these were the short and to-the-point ways of summing up how the man was viewed by those around him, and how he saw himself and found his own sense of identity.

The man came to Jesus with what may be the most important question ever articulated by any person. He was asking the right question, and he was addressing it to the right person. The man inquired, "What must I do to inherit eternal life?" He was, in effect, asking Jesus to lay out the plan of salvation. The response that Jesus gave is fascinating. He did not provide the man with a Roman Road formula for salvation. He did not give four spiritual laws. He did not lead the man through a blind progression of small steps to get to a decision.

Here is what Jesus said to the rich, young ruler. He laid out a three-part demand on him. Interestingly, the three elements of Jesus' requirement of the man correspond exactly to the threefold way in which the Gospel writer described him. Jesus said, "Sell all that you own and distribute the money to the poor, and you will have treasure in heaven: then come, follow me" (Luke 18:22). These actions addressed the three areas of pride and self-worship that separated this young man from a relationship with God.

He was devoted to his wealth; therefore, Jesus said, "Sell all that you own." The man was caught in the web of his own narcissism, so Jesus said, "Get the focus of your life off yourself by seeing and feeling compassion for the poor." The man was proud of his position of influence and power, so Jesus said, "You must leave behind the worship of power by submitting yourself to my lordship and becoming a devoted follower of mine."

This is not the plan of salvation given other places in Scripture. It is not to be understood as a general principle of how people come to receive eternal life. This was a specific message directed to the individual circumstances of a unique human being. There may be many others who identify with the rich, young ruler, and for whom the message Jesus had for him is very relevant, but the conversation was personal and custom-fit to this young man.

Jesus knew the niche. He cared enough about wealthy, young influentials to verbalize his message in ways that were meaningful and relevant to their needs.

The Niche:
Prosperous but Lonely, Social Outcasts

Another encounter of Jesus, recorded in Luke 19, is with a man named Zacchaeus. This man lived in the city of Jericho, and he made his living as a tax collector. The Roman Empire collected taxes from the people of all of the occupied nations over which they ruled. Jews, much to their chagrin, paid taxes to Rome. To facilitate the collection of these taxes, the Roman government employed Jewish citizens to serve as revenue agents of Rome. This was Rome's "External Revenue Service."

These tax collectors extracted money from their own fellow citizens. They were often viewed as traitors, paid by Rome with a commission or a percentage based on what they collected. The more they were able to squeeze out of their friends and neighbors, the happier they made the Roman officials, and the more prosperous they became. Zacchaeus was the chief tax collector in the Jericho district. He was enormously wealthy and lived comfortably in a beautiful mansion surrounded by a high wall. His home was filled with works of art and tasteful furnishings, but he had few visitors. He was despised by his countrymen.

Zacchaeus was not only short on friends, he was short of stature. When word came to him that Jesus was coming his way, he realized that he had no chance to see Jesus without some help. He needed an advantage. He discovered that just as his relationship with the Roman government gave him an economic edge, he could use a sycamore tree to compensate for being vertically challenged.

So, here was this man who was among the least popular in town, the man with the beautiful home and appointments but no friends with whom to share them. Jesus spotted him perched in the tree. Jesus spoke. He did not preach a sermon of sin and redemption to Zacchaeus. He did not rebuke him for his betrayal of his own people. He did not comment on what a short, downhill road to hell Zacchaeus was traveling.

Jesus said, "Zacchaeus, hurry and come down; for I must stay at your house today" (Luke 19:5). Was that not a poignant remark to make to the loneliest man in town? Had not Zacchaeus longed for someone, anyone, to show an interest in seeing his place? Did he not ache to show his prize possessions to someone who might respond with something other than an insult?

Jesus did not begin his relationship with Zacchaeus by commanding him to sell all and give to the poor. It is interesting to note, however, that the outcome of this relationship was that Zacchaeus chose to dispose of half of his possessions and give to the poor. He further committed that he would repay any whom he had defrauded by a factor of four. So Zacchaeus was converted because Jesus cared enough to sense the deep longing of his heart, to go out of his way to minister to that emptiness, and to relate to the person that proper society had rejected.

Jesus, the niche marketing natural, made contact with a niche others overlooked. He spoke the language and bridged the barriers to touch a hurting soul. He made a house call. Jesus used this occasion to reaffirm and state very succinctly his life purpose: "The Son of Man came to seek out and to save the lost" (Luke 19:10).

The Niche:
Persons Suffering from the Effects of Severe Moral Failure

Most of John 4 is devoted to the story of the Samaritan woman whom Jesus encountered at the well in Sychar. This woman had known a rough life. She had been married five times, and at the time of this chance meeting with a Jewish stranger, she was living with a man to whom she was not married. Her story was one of failed relationships, moral indiscretions, and social disgrace. She was at the well, which was called Jacob's well, in the middle of the day. Some biblical commentators say that the standard time for women to go to the town well was in the early morning. They would go to secure the household supply of water for drinking and cooking for the day. Those women, however, who were of poor reputation, might go to the well at midday when others were not present, thus avoiding the condemning stares and the snide remarks of the proper women of the town. This was such a woman. Jesus, being thirsty but having no vessel with which to draw from the well, asked the woman for a drink.

More immediate, in her mind, than responding to his simple request was the need to know who this man was and why he dared address her. She was shocked that a Jewish man would be seen speaking to a Samaritan woman. Jesus was flaunting several social norms. Men did not interact with women in public, Jews did not speak with Samaritans, and no socially respectable person had dealings with persons who were known to be morally disreputable. She expressed her curiosity about Jesus' forwardness in speaking to her. His immediate message to her was, "If you knew the gift of God, and who it is that is saying to you, 'Give me a drink,' you would have asked him, and he would have given you living water" (John 4:10). Here is the Gospel as Jesus articulated it for the woman at the well. This woman, whose life was characterized by a frantic search for satisfaction of a deep thirst of her spirit, was being offered water that would quench that longing. Jesus helped her to recognize that her serial relationships were not satisfying the real thirst, and that only a deep spiritual experience would fill her need.

The woman attempted to divert the subject of their conversation from the need in her life, to a debate about the proper traditions and places for worship. She wanted to avoid the painful process of dealing with her own spiritual dryness by engaging in a theological argument. Finally, the woman affirmed that she did believe that eventually a Messiah would come. Jesus, undeterred by her efforts to avoid dealing with the larger issues, made one of the clearest declarations of his identity to be found in the New Testament. Jesus said, "I am he, the one who is speaking to you" (John 4:26). She not only came to believe that fact, but she became a bold and convincing witness to others about the salvation she had found in Christ.

Jesus cared about a person for whom others expressed contempt. He recognized the spiritual thirst that had dominated her life, and he offered living water to satisfy her longing. Jesus understood the persons who occupied this niche.

The Niche:
The Untouchables

Leprosy, in biblical times, was a death sentence. But worse than just a terminal illness, it was degenerative in a way that allowed the sufferer to see daily evidence of what was being lost. And even more tragic than the physical effects, it was degenerative in terms of all human relationships. Lepers were made to live in isolation to avoid infecting others. They were separated from family and friends, and they were forced to warn others to stay away from them by shouting, "Unclean! Unclean!" when they walked down a city street.

These were the untouchables. The rules against touching lepers were religious rules forbidding Jews touching unclean things, social rules that made it a cultural taboo, and legal rules based on the concern to prevent contagion. Finally, common sense reminded most people that one simply does not ever want to touch a leper; therefore, lepers were persons who never experienced the pleasant sensation of human touch. They lived an isolated, miserable, lonely existence.

In Luke 5:12-16, a leper approached Jesus with a bold expression of faith, saying, "Lord, if you choose, you can make me clean" (v. 12). Jesus responded immediately and healed the man. He spoke the words of healing, and that surely would have been sufficient to accomplish the task, but before he spoke, he did something more dramatic and meaningful. He touched the man. He touched him! He touched an untouchable.

This is the way with Jesus, the Son of God. He knew that no word or gesture would be as powerful to a leper as the amazing experience of being touched by another person. Jesus understood the depth of the pain and longing of this leper, and he chose to communicate with the man by providing for the greatest felt need in the leper's life.

The Niche:
Persons with Crippling Dependencies

One day, as Jesus made his way into Jerusalem, he passed a public pool of water that was used for watering animals (John 5). A legend had grown up around this particular pool, which claimed that at certain times, an angel would stir the water. The first ill person who could get into the water when it was troubled, the legend held, would be healed. Therefore, many of the lame persons of the city spent their days lying on the porticoes that surrounded this pool.

On this day, as Jesus approached the area, his gaze fixed on one disabled man who had been in his condition nearly 40 years. What would his first words be to this disabled man? How could he express God's love for a man whose life circumstance gave him little reason to believe in a God of love? What kind of comfort could Jesus express? What words of sympathy or hope would he speak?

Jesus spoke. He looked at the man and said, "Do you want to be made well?" (John 5:6). What? What kind of question is that to ask someone who has suffered with a terrible disability for 40 years?

Jesus knew it was the right question. He understood that sometimes people come to depend on their dependencies. It is possible for a person to need his or her disability more than the person needs or desires healing and wholeness. The disability may excuse a great deal of dependent behavior. It may provide the sufferer with a sense of identity as a victim and as a person who cannot be held responsible. This tendency to cling to our disabilities may apply to those of us who deal with spiritual and emotional challenges, as well as to those who have physical challenges. So this was precisely the right question for this man.

Proving how on target Jesus was with his query, the man refused to answer that direct question. He responded with his victim speech about how he could never get to the pool quickly enough because he had no one to help him. Jesus then gave him the direct command, "Stand up, take your mat and walk" (John 5:8). Seems like a tough-love approach does it not? There is no indication that Jesus spoke words of encouragement to the man. Nothing indicates that he reached out to help him to his feet for the first time in nearly 40 years.

Jesus understood the specific set of needs that the man had. He fashioned his approach to the man based on the compassion of saying what the man needed to hear, rather than what he wanted to hear. He asked the question that helped the man to see that as dependent as he was on others for physical necessities, he had allowed himself to become even more dependent in his mind and emotions. Jesus healed the physical disability, but he also addressed the spiritual and emotional needs that held the key to complete wholeness.

Moving from Intuitive Wisdom to a Logical Process

What we discover when we look at Jesus' ministry is that many of the principles from secular marketing are indeed appropriate to the task of evangelism. The key is to keep in mind that the reason we are working to reach people is not to make money for shareholders, but to share the good news that God loves us. This book is my effort to take what Jesus and others have done intuitively and provide a system for applying those principles in everyday practice. There will be offered, in this volume, a process that follows sound marketing principles to accomplish similar effectiveness in ministry. It is my fervent hope that the reader will find useful tools for greater effectiveness.

Because of the cross-disciplinary nature of this task, some terms commonly used in marketing may not be applicable or appropriate in congregational growth, and vice versa. I will, therefore, provide in this introduction an explanation of terms that may be used. It is a little unusual to begin a book with a glossary, but given the nature of the broad sweep of this book, it seems appropriate. Some of the words and phrases listed below are from business administration, and others are more uniquely related to the field of congregational growth. This glossary, like the book itself, is an effort to create a common vocabulary that will serve to bridge the communication gap between the two disciplines of business marketing and congregational outreach strategizing.

It will prove worth the time invested up front to get a sense of the marketing terms that will be encountered in this book. In many instances, the terms are logical, and common sense provides an adequate definition. In some cases, everyone has a concept of what the term means, but it is helpful to define it more precisely for the purposes of this book.

One exception to my use of marketing terms in the context of congregations is my discomfort with the word *target* to describe a segment to be addressed. I will generally attempt to avoid it in this book. The reason is that for congregational life, the persons who are the focus of our outreach efforts are precious souls for whom God loves. A target sometimes implies an impersonal thing that is to be acted upon. It may even be something to be shot at. I would not want to be understood as diminishing the value or personhood of any individual or group for the sake of congregational growth. It should also be noted that the *prospect* (another term I am not crazy about) for our outreach is not just someone to be acted upon. The person is an active participant in whatever decisions or actions are made with regard to a relationship with God and with a congregation. Rather than the term *target*, I will attempt to speak of *niche groups*, the focus of our efforts, the customer, or the unreached person. The term *target group* or *target marketing* may appear in direct quotes of other authors.

The following glossary is provided also because a number of important congregational growth concepts are expressed in the descriptions of the terms that are listed here.

Marketing Terms to Know

Advertising: Any type of media-delivered communication about goods or services that is paid for by the organization sponsoring the communication. Advertising may have a variety of purposes: to let people know that the product or organization exists, to create brand-name recognition, to create positive images or goodwill for the product or organization, to sell the product, to enlist or recruit a customer, to reinforce the decision of the person who is already a customer, to create brand loyalty, and so forth.

Bait and switch: This is the unscrupulous advertising practice of offering a special deal on a product, but when the customer arrives to buy it, the product is not available and the vendor attempts to sell one that is not such a good deal.

Customer: The consumer of a product or a service; the person toward whom advertising and marketing efforts are directed. In the congregational context, the customer may be the unenlisted person whom the congregation is attempting to reach, or it may be the active member whom the congregation hopes to serve. The decision about who is its customer is a key matter to be decided by the leaders of every congregation. If the primary customer is the person who is already an involved member of the organization, marketing and outreach methodologies may be irrelevant.

Demographics: Statistical data about a given population. It is usually based on census information and may include statistical analysis of an area by zip code, census tract, or other geographic or sociological division. Typically the information provided includes: age, sex, marital status, birthrate, mortality rate, education level, income, housing type (rented or owned, single family or multifamily) and occupation.

Focus Group: A personal interview technique in which a group of 6 to 12 persons may be brought together to be questioned about their ideas or views on an issue, idea, or product. The focus group may be formed within the organization's membership, or it may be randomly or selectively enlisted from outside the organization. Outside focus groups often have to be paid or in some way compensated for their time.

Market driven: An organizational orientation based on an understanding of the population of actual and potential customers for the product or service offered. This principle of being market driven may influence how planning, strategizing, and visioning for the future are done.

Marketing: A management philosophy that recognizes that the customer is the focal point of the activity of an organization, as is the activity of appealing to the customer to enlist his or her consumption of a product or utilization of a service.

Market Segmentation: The process of breaking down a large, diverse market into small, more homogeneous segments, with the possibility of a different advertising or marketing process being utilized for each segment.

Observational Research: A research method that involves observing and recording people's behavior, but avoiding direct interaction.

Positioning: A process through which a marketer establishes with a customer a distinct place for his or her product or service within the customer's mind.

Sample: A group of persons who are representative of a larger population being surveyed.

Seekers: Persons who may or may not be actively attending a religious organization, but who are engaged in spiritual thought and exploration. They have an interest and openness to developing a more satisfying spirituality.

Shopping-Mall Intercept: An interview approach that involves approaching or intercepting individuals at a particular spot in a shopping mall and asking them questions designed to secure information for marketing purposes.

Specialty Store (or Boutique Store): A retail store for which customers develop a strong preference due to the particular product or service offered or the perceived quality of what is provided.

Target: A person or group of persons toward which marketing efforts are directed.

Telephone Interview: A survey method that involves phoning, either randomly or selectively, to question respondents on a given issue.

Unchurched: Persons who may be able to state a religious or denominational preference, but who have not attended a place of worship in the previous six months other than for a wedding or funeral.

1

Hope for the Struggling Congregation
Find a Niche and Scratch It!

These days, when a family moves to a community or for whatever reason decides that they are interested in finding a place of worship and spiritual nurture, they will visit several congregations in their area. The idea of driving 15 minutes, or even 25 minutes, to find a congregation that offers what they are looking for is no discouragement whatsoever in their ultimate choice. If they have children, they want excellent programs and leadership for children. If they are empty nesters, they want full programs and possibilities for persons in their circumstance. If they are middle-class, they want the congregation to reflect the same comforts, conveniences, and decor they are accustomed to enjoying at home. In most cases, the smaller congregations they visit simply cannot exhibit the range and depth of offerings that the larger congregation can.

In my work as a church consultant, I have been in dozens of congregations in the past 15 years in which the average age of the typical Sunday morning congregation is at least 60. Many of the active and financially supportive members of these congregations are past 75 years of age. It does not require great wisdom or foresight to recognize that these congregations are in serious trouble.

Many fine communities of faith, with great heritages and resources, are struggling with changing communities and aging memberships at the dawn of the 21st century. The past 10 years have been especially difficult for communities of faith that have fewer than 300 members or Sunday morning attendance numbers of fewer than 150. These would be congregations generally classified as smaller and midsize. The same challenges are encountered whether the settings of these congregations are rural or urban. All are finding life increasingly difficult.

As much as we dislike the word *competition* used in the context of the reign of God, the fact is that we live in an environment where competition

15

is a reality, even for souls enlisted in congregational involvement. There are many factors that make the challenges greater for midsize and smaller congregations in this postmodern age. I will only attempt to mention a few.

1. **Cultural changes.** The time in which we live is called postmodern, and some refer to it as post-Christian. This terminology is a way of observing that the prevailing culture no longer holds a mainline religious worldview. The United States, if it ever was properly called a Christian nation, can no longer be understood as a place where the cultural environment is strongly encouraging of those who regularly attend their church, synagogue, or mosque, and who try to live faithfully to their understanding of the will of God. A cursory review of the popular culture will confirm that what we watch on television, see at the movies, read in the magazines, and discuss at the office is much less "church friendly" than it was 20 years ago.

2. **An aging congregational membership.** As mentioned above, the typical smaller congregation is watching its core membership become elderly. The adults who were reached in the 1960s and '70s, the glory years for many mainstream Christian denominations, are now in their autumn years. They were the strength of small congregations for the last quarter of the 20th century, but now they are passing from the scene.

3. **The emergence of the megachurch as a national and international phenomenon.** In most communities of any size these days, there is at least one congregation that has a regular attendance of over 500 persons. In many places, there are even larger megachurches within five miles of struggling smaller congregations, megachurches that may regularly have several thousand worshipers. These congregations usually have large ministry staffs, a broad range of programs and offerings, excellent age-level ministries, outstanding music, and the finest of facilities. The small and midsize congregations in the area simply cannot compete with the megachurch in the scope and overall quality of the programs and ministries it is able to offer.

4. **A "survival" mentality that sets in with the smaller congregation when it is in decline.** When a congregation shifts from the pursuit of its God-given mission to an obsession with its own survival, it becomes something less than a church. It is altogether understandable that a congregation might feel hurt and at risk when it is rejected over and over by people who visit when they are looking for a new church. Let the driving passion for the church always be to serve and to give itself to the cause of

reaching people with the message of God's love. The drive to reach people simply so that they may become contributors to the survival of the institution is not an adequate or an effective motivation for congregation growth.

5. A resistance to change. One of the reasons smaller congregations are failing is not that they are small in number, but that they are small in their openness to following the movement of the Spirit of God. Our God is dynamic and creative. God is constantly doing new things and inspiring new life; therefore, the people of God have every reason to be about that appreciation of newness. New ideas, new methods, and new ministries can give vitality and excitement in the smaller congregation the same as they can in the larger one. In his study of the church, George Barna, a popular religious researcher and writer, discovered that "Christians and churches make two types of blunders when it comes to handling change: They refuse to change when change is called for, or they 'change for the sake of change' resulting in indefensible and inappropriate decisions."[1]

6. A lack of sensitivity to the people around them. Throughout the United States, there are congregations declining and losing vitality, yet there are people who are experiencing enormous pain and emptiness living within a few miles of the congregations. Smaller congregations are often the most compassionate when there is a death in the community or a house fire or a tragedy. But these same congregation members are strangely silent and inactive when a crying need exists for childcare for working single moms, or healthcare for the poor, or transportation for senior citizens, or tutoring for underprivileged children. Much of society has come to see the church as irrelevant, because they do not perceive that it is hearing the cries or seeing the need or caring about the pain of the world. Unchurched people often seem to be saying to us, "You don't care about me; I don't care about you."

A very dire prediction of what lies ahead for traditional, mainline congregations is offered by author Mike Regele. Regele is the cofounder and president of Percept Group, Inc., an organization that provides demographic and marketing studies for interested congregations. In his book, ominously entitled *Death of the Church*, he says, "A decision is imminent, but it is only a decision about *how* the church will die. Death is inescapable. We cannot and will not avoid it. The institutional church will either choose to die or it will choose to die in order to live."[2] Regele offers two possible futures for congregations. One is the slow, painful death of gradual decline due to resistance to change and creeping irrelevance. The other is the sacrificial, Christ-like death of giving up one's life in order to know a new and more spiritually vital quality of existence.

It is this second kind of death that holds the hope for the future of congregations. It is not saying that everything must change or that all tradition and custom must be thrown out. It is, however, calling for a commitment to cultural relevance and relationship building that will allow churches to consider new paradigms of structure, method, and approach. The congregation must be open to reinventing itself. In circumstances where traditional methods are effective, they may be reaffirmed. But in situations where the methods of the past do not work, there must be a commitment to experimentation and innovation. As one wag has put it, "When the horse is dead, it is time to dismount."

The Small Congregation:
A Boutique Rather Than a "Mom and Pop"

Bob Dale, in his book *Leadership for a Changing Church*, makes the following statement about the different circumstances encountered by congregations in our time:

> Years ago most local churches mirrored their community and ministered to a crossroads gathering point, a village or a neighborhood. From a marketing perspective, these congregations functioned like a family business in a mixed market. But times have changed. . . . The trend in marketing is moving from mass marketing to niche marketing.[3]

The challenges facing small and midsize congregations do have analogies in the secular world of business enterprise. Across the country, the proliferation of Wal-Mart, Kmart, and other similar discount stores offering nearly everything a shopper needs to buy with one-stop shopping, has led to the demise of the small, locally owned store dealing in hardware, sporting goods, toys, clothing, automotive supplies, or lawn and garden needs. Hundreds of communities have witnessed the closing of these smaller stores that could not compete with the high volume, discounted pricing, and high visibility of the larger store chains. It would lead one to conclude that bigger is always better, and is, in fact, the only way to survive.

But go down the street from Wal-Mart or Kmart to the new mall that was built within the last five years. What do you find lining the walkways of the mall? Small stores—and hundreds of them. They are highly specialized, very narrow in scope, and clearly identified with a particular product. There are stores like "Things Remembered" or "Now 'n' Then" that sell things that can be engraved. There are even smaller stores that are dotted throughout the mall in gazebos. These portable stores may be selling only watches, only cell phones, only knives and swords, or only neckties. So while mom-and-pop stores are going the way of the dinosaur, other small, specialized retail operations are making money and growing.

What makes the difference? What is unique and significant about these boutique operations? Obviously, they are very focused on doing one thing. They do not expect to sell to everyone entering the mall. They have in mind the specific customer who has an interest in buying a watch or a tie or a bonsai tree on this trip to the store. The customer may enter the mall with the purchase in mind, or be vulnerable to impulse buying. The specialty stores have a very clear sense of what they offer, who their customer is, and how to best meet the customer for a quick transaction. They tend to be efficient, and they count on the networking benefit of being in proximity to other stores that are viewed as complementary to their offerings rather than directly competitive. The mall boutiques tend to be more upscale, so their market niche may include persons who are more interested in convenience and quality than in the lowest price in town.

These boutique stores appear not only in malls, but in renovated downtown areas and in the city-center developments that are showing up across the country. Their success gives some clues to how small and midsize congregations can flourish in this new world, but even more significantly, their success gives hope to smaller congregations. Indeed, one of the saddest realities about the mindset of smaller congregations is that they often have been beaten down by years of perceiving that they were failing, while other congregations around them were succeeding. Hope for a meaningful future becomes a viable possibility. Jeremiah 29:11 says, "I know the plans I have for you, says the Lord, plans for your welfare and not for harm, to give you a future with hope." That reassurance of God's help and good intentions for God's people reminds us that we need never abandon hope for accomplishing those things that are within God's purposes for us. Certainly if small businesses, small stores, and small service organizations can prosper in our culture, then small and midsize congregations can as well. If these congregations have a strong sense of their purpose within God's redemptive enterprise, if they are willing to learn their strengths and the needs of their community, and if they are sensitive to the leadership of the Spirit of God, they can find ways to fulfill their highest and noblest calling.

The Small and Midsize Congregation: Building on Strength

There has been an ongoing debate among church growth experts about whether plateaued and declining congregations should build on their strengths or concentrate on correcting their glaring weaknesses. If asked, "Should my congregations build on its strengths or find and correct its weaknesses?" the best answer is yes. It would be unwise to follow either approach to the neglect of the other. Congregations should certainly know, value, and continue to take advantage of their unique strengths, resources, and possibilities. But congregations must also give attention to the wide gaps that may exist in their congregational life. The besetting weakness may overwhelm all of the good that could be done by majoring on strengths. Conversely, the congregation can spend too much time bemoaning and trying to cover its weaknesses, and in so doing neglect the very qualities that make it desirable and effective.

Lyle Schaller is one of America's best known and most influential church consultants, and he is the author of more than 40 books on congregational effectiveness. In an article in *Net Results* magazine entitled "Responding to the Competition," Schaller offers three basic suggestions for congregations wishing to assess their growth potential:

1. **Study the Competition!** Schaller suggests that congregation leaders visit other congregations to discover what they are doing that is working.

2. **Engage in Self-Appraisal.** Congregations should look at who they have been successful in reaching, what methods have worked well for them and how they can expand those efforts.

3. **Increase the Entry Points.** In order to increase the effectiveness of outreach, congregations should attempt to create more and better ways of building relationships and receiving new people.[4]

As a congregation attempts to discover how it can best address opportunities for increased ministry in its area, one of the first questions to ask itself is, "What do we do well?" The appeal for new people to become involved can best be based on letting guests see the unique strengths and best qualities the congregation has to offer.

Applying Marketing Principles to Congregational Growth

The term used in marketing circles for identifying and focusing efforts on specific segments of the population is *market segmentation* or *niche marketing*. This approach holds possibilities for congregations. For many years, Schaller has been speaking and writing about the need for congregations to utilize a planning method which he has called *market-driven planning*.

George Barna has said, "The church of the future must be a community of faith that facilitates highly personalized and focused ministry." In his book, *The Second Coming of the Church*, Barna states, "Most churches contend that they must have something for everyone. We have come to believe that every church must take care of every need of every person who might ever have any interaction with the organization."[5] Schaller and Barna and many others are telling us that congregations must sharpen their focus and become clearer about the unique ministries they can offer to address the unique needs that exist in their area.

This utilization of the best principles of secular marketing in the outreach and enlistment efforts of the congregation holds the promise of making a significant difference in the future of many congregations. For small and midsize congregations, this approach may provide the best hope for life and effectiveness in the 21st century. These ideas, however, are not just useful to small and midsize congregations. Large congregations as well can open new markets, reach new people, and become even more effective by giving attention to the lessons to be learned from secular marketing disciplines. Every congregation that is motivated to grow will be interested in identifying its niches and developing better ways of relating to those people who have been neglected and ignored by faith communities in their area. Your congregation can find a niche and scratch it.

2

Where Do We Have the Muscle?

N o congregation can be totally competent in all areas of its work. The faith community that has excellent worship and music may lack in the quality of its educational programs. A congregation that does an excellent job of reaching new people may fall short in the process of assimilating them. Even the thriving megachurches can usually identify an area of the total scope of congregational enterprise where they need to do a better job. This is equally true of midsize and smaller congregations.

This chapter deals with the possibility of leveraging congregational strengths to achieve greater outreach. But before discussing the assessment of organizational strengths, it will be helpful to consider some of the common weaknesses of today's congregations.

Much has been written about the importance of healthy organizations being learning organizations. In that sense, much of what goes wrong with congregations could be called learning disabilities.

All Congregations Have Weaknesses

One learning disability is *contextual dyslexia*. One of the essential skills for a congregation during a time of rapid social change is the ability to read its context. Unfortunately, many congregations are out of touch with the environment in which they exist. There are two primary causes for this inability to read the culture. Some congregations are at war with the popular culture or with the particular culture of those who live in their immediate community. They express nothing but criticism and contempt for what they see going on around them. These congregations have little hope of reaching unchurched persons because they do not love, or even like, those who are at home in popular culture.

The second reason congregations may fail to read their context is because they are blissfully ignorant of the societal changes and cultural shifts that are taking place. As styles of dress, forms of entertainment, attitudes toward minorities, and other cultural norms change, some of those most active in faith communities remain out of touch with these shifts. These congregations are living in a state of denial, believing that if they ignore the changes, the date will remain 1955. Many mainline religious groups had their glory days in the 1960s and '70s when a 1950s worldview was not that far out of touch. The evidence of whether a congregation is stuck in a 1950s worldview is to see to what degree their worship, discipleship, evangelism, and other congregational programs have changed in the past 50 years.

Speech impediments are another form of disability. Some congregations lack the ability to speak their message clearly and understandably. This is often a problem of vocabulary. Like all organizations with a long tradition, congregations tend to develop an insider vocabulary that communicates well to those who know the code, but that sounds like gibberish to the outsider. These well-intentioned congregations put the burden for understanding on the hearer. They may say, "We are putting the message out, but 'those people' just won't listen." Congregations that are truly interested in communicating with the unchurched make deliberate efforts to learn to speak in ways the unchurched can understand. The congregation assumes that if the message is not getting through, it is not the problem of the hearer; it is the responsibility of the speaker to find better ways of communicating the message.

Hyperactivity is a problem that congregations can experience. They become so busy doing the many tasks required to maintain the institution that they have no time to focus on the primary mission. Congregations often wear out their active members doing committee work and administrative functions, then wonder why no one is engaged in outreach and ministry. Sometimes congregations develop short attention spans in the process of their overactivity, so that outreach plans are not carried out.

In his book, *The Second Coming of the Church*, George Barna identifies three primary causes for the failure of congregations these days. That failure often takes the form of declining membership and attendance, a lack of energy for engaging in ministry or a pessimistic attitude toward the future. He notes that these three problems are dealt with in the letters to the churches, as recorded in Revelation. Barna writes that congregations fail when they "lose focus" on the primary mission that they have been given. The church in Ephesus was accused of abandoning their first love, their devotion to Jesus Christ (Rev. 2:1-7). A second cause for failure, according to Barna, is when churches "lose their passion" for doing ministry with energy and zeal. The church in Sardis is said to have lost its vitality; it had a reputation of being alive, but it was dead (Rev. 3:14-22). The third problem Barna notes is that churches "lose sight of their common enemy." The church of Pergamum was experiencing division and conflict because of efforts to embrace diversity without keeping in mind the common enemy of the pervasive evil that all people of God must face (Rev. 2:12-17).[1]

Assessing the Strengths of Our Congregation

Market-driven approaches to congregational growth involve being realistic about what a congregation can and cannot reasonably expect to accomplish. Every congregation is unique, and each one is uniquely gifted to accomplish the purposes of God in its geographic area and time in history. An important aspect of the effort to determine how a congregation can be most effective is to honestly assess the strengths of the congregation. This is an internal study of what the congregation is presently doing well. There are numerous ways of gathering data with regard to the strengths of the congregation.

Existing Records of the Congregation

Most congregations keep records of membership, attendance, giving, and other such basic statistics. Some of the elements of strength in the congregation can be gleaned from the study of these records. Among the questions that may be answered by this information are:

1. Has the congregation been growing in its membership?
2. Has the increase been primarily by transfer from other congregations or by baptism or confirmation?
3. In the past five years, has the congregation had a net increase or a net

decrease in the number of resident (those living within a reasonable commuting distance of the congregation) members?

4. In what age brackets (groupings by decade) has the congregation experienced growth or a lack of growth?

5. In what age brackets has the congregation experienced a loss of members?

6. Do the records indicate the nature of the loss of members (death, transfer, etc.)?

7. Has worship attendance been growing?

8. Has Bible study attendance been growing?

9. Has giving been increasing?

10. If so, has the congregation seen an increase in the number of giving units or in the amount given per unit?

11. What specific programs of the congregation seem to be growing?

12. What programs of the congregation appear to be declining?

13. Are social activities better attended now than they were five years ago?

14. What new groups (Bible studies, musical groups, support groups, etc.) have been formed in the past five years?

15. What new ministries have been started in the past five years?

A congregation may benefit from the assistance of an outside consultant for help interpreting the answers to these questions. The objectivity and expertise of a qualified congregational consultant can help put meaning to the raw data that is gathered. There will be suggestions and examples to help with this task of interpreting data later in this book.

Aids Created from the Records

The statistical records can be utilized to create helpful summary materials that give the congregation a better sense of its strengths. One question to ask is, "What kind of people have we been effective in reaching?" Another is, "Where do they come from geographically?"

A pin map is a helpful way to see the specific geographic neighborhoods from which members are coming. Congregation leaders may secure a large map of the area in which members of the congregation live. The congregation records should indicate the names and addresses of members. Each of those addresses can be located on the map, and a colored stickpin should be placed there. There are professional market-research organizations that will provide this kind of map based on a congregation's directory. The process is called geocoding. This service can be expensive, however, and there may be value in having congregation members work together to produce the pin map. Their hands-on involvement gives them a stronger sense of ownership of the process and a clearer understanding of the results.

It is most helpful to utilize a system of colored pins, with the various colors meaning different things in terms of when or by what process the person joined the congregation. A possible scheme might be:

- red pins: members who joined more than 20 years ago
- blue pins: members who joined 10 to 20 years ago
- green pins: members who joined 5 to 10 years ago
- yellow pins: members who joined in the past 5 years
- white pins: persons who registered as visitors to the congregation in the past 6 months

Once completed, a map of this type can be helpful to a congregation's understanding of where its people are coming from, and whether there has been any shift in the areas from which members are being drawn. The clusters of colored pins can show a great deal about the nature of the congregation and its potential growth. It is always helpful to have several leaders of the congregation study the map and discuss their observations. The group process is particularly useful in analyzing and gaining insight into the wisdom that can come from such a study of the congregation.

Another form of visual representation of a congregation's self study is the use of graphs and charts. Among the information that may be helpful to graph are such statistical measurements as:

- congregation membership for the past 10 to 20 years
- average weekly worship attendance for the past 10 to 20 years
- number of baptisms or confirmations for the past 10 to 20 years
- number of persons transferring membership from other congregations for the past 10 to 20 years
- number of Sunday morning visitors in services for the past 2 years
- total giving to the congregation's budget for the past 10 to 20 years
- numbers of persons involved in major ministries of the congregation for the past 10 to 20 years

These charts and graphs may be developed by looking up the numbers and plotting them. As with many congregation processes, however, it is desirable to have a group working together. The sharing of ideas and the joint wisdom of several perspectives will usually produce a better product. Decisions will need to be made about the best format for visually displaying the information. In some cases, a simple line on a graph may suffice. In other instances, a bar graph, a pie chart, or some other type of chart may be the most effective. The decision of which format to use should be based on what visual aid will best help the average member of the congregation to understand and remember the information being shared.

Member Questionnaires

No internal study of a congregation can be complete without providing every interested member an opportunity to participate. A written questionnaire, for example, is one of the most efficient ways of securing valuable information from members. Such a survey might include demographic information about members to determine the marital status, education level, economic status, profession, and other similar data. This information will be useful in comparing the demographic and lifestyle characteristics of the congregation with the community it seeks to serve.

The value of a written survey or questionnaire, however, depends on the care and skill with which it is designed, administered, and evaluated. A helpful summary of the basic principles involved in questionnaire design is provided in *The Portable MBA in Marketing*, a primer in marketing written by Alexander Hiam and Charles Schewe. This summary says, "All questions should be as easy to answer as possible. . . . Personal questions . . . should only be asked if necessary. . . . Care should be taken to use simple and unambiguous words and phrases."[2]

The book goes on to list some of the questioning techniques that can be used:

1.   Likert scale: This is a form of questioning that provides respondents with a statement and asks them to indicate the extent to which they agree or disagree with the statement. Responses will typically be: "strongly agree, moderately agree, no opinion, moderately disagree, strongly disagree." This type of question is simple for the respondent, and it provides answers that can be easily counted and compiled. Example: I believe our congregation is growing (respond on agree/disagree scale).

2. Semantic differential: This technical term refers to a method of asking people to mark their level of feeling about a question on a continuum. The ends of the scales are bipolar terms expressing the extremes of possible responses. For example,

I believe our church is:

Friendly	-------------------------------------	Unfriendly
Growing	-------------------------------------	Declining
Enthusiastic	-------------------------------------	Complacent

3. Word association: Respondents are given a list of words and asked to record the first word or phrase that comes to mind when they consider each one. The instruction might read, "What is the first word that comes to mind when you hear the following?"

Worship _____

Christian education _____

Stewardship _____

4. Sentence completion: Incomplete sentences are given, and respondents are asked to complete them in a way that expresses their attitude or opinion. This is a very open-ended way of surveying views, but it is also more difficult to quantify and score. The advantage of open-ended questions, however, is that respondents may provide more information than can be gleaned with short-answer or multiple-choice responses. Example:

a. When I joined this congregation, I was most impressed by

_____

b. If our congregation had to relocate, I think we should move to

_____

5.   Importance scale: This is a scale that rates things on a scale from "not at all important" to "extremely important." Example: How important is it to you that our church has a printed worship folder on Sunday mornings?

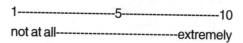

6.   Rating scale: This method rates on a scale similar to the one listed above in number five, but the bipolar points are "extremely poor" and "excellent." Example: Discipleship education in our church is:

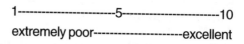

Questionnaires can be used to get both quantitative and qualitative research data. Quantitative information is factual, objective, and usually involves short, exact responses. Qualitative information will be more conceptual, subjective, and complex. It allows for assessment of feelings, opinions, and beliefs. The types of questions and the way in which they are asked will determine which kind of information is obtained.

The design of a questionnaire should involve finding answers to questions such as:

- What do we need to learn?
- Who should we ask in order to learn it?
- What is our best way to get a response from those we seek to question? When and where can we contact them?
- How should we ask the questions to get the most reliable responses?
- How will the responses be compiled and evaluated?
- What will we do with the information we secure?

Inside Focus Groups

A focus group is a group of 6 to 12 persons who are brought together to be interviewed in a discussion format. They may be asked to share their opinions, ideas, or attitudes about issues of interest to the convening organization. In marketing research, the focus groups may be formed within the organization or made up of people outside the organization, depending on the nature of what the researchers are trying to learn. Focus groups can be a useful tool in a congregation doing a self-study to determine its strengths.

An important aspect of maximizing the value of the focus group is planning the questions to be raised with the group. Typically the facilitator of the group will be prepared with 8 to 12 topics for discussion. The issues to be discussed should be carefully worded to avoid manipulating or influencing the responses. People will often attempt to give the answers that leaders seem to want to hear. If the issues can be skillfully introduced enabling open and free discussion, the things learned from the group process will be more useful. The questions asked or issues raised should reflect the specific areas of information the researchers hope to learn, without being too obvious.

Chapter 3 contains examples of the use of an inside focus group at University Heights Baptist Church, a midsize congregation in Springfield, Missouri. Chapter 4 reports on an external focus group project that was conducted in preparation for a new church start in the suburbs of Richmond, Virginia. This new congregation, RiverSouth Community Church, was begun with a core group of about 20 persons, and with careful research to understand the culture of the area where the church planned to locate. That chapter will include detailed information to explain how the outside focus group was formed, how the topics for discussion were planned and worded, and how the group was conducted.

Most of the principles and approaches are similar for an inside focus group. One difference is that it is much easier to get attendance and cooperation from an internal group. Very often, people invited to an outside focus group need to be paid cash or otherwise compensated for giving their time. Generally, members of a congregation will give time to the effort simply as a way of supporting and assisting their congregation.

One of the tasks in holding inside focus groups is the enlisting of the congregation's members as participants. The following page contains the instructions developed for enlisting inside focus group participants at University Heights Church.

Informational Meeting
Enlisting New Members for Focus Groups
University Heights Baptist Church

Focus Group Meeting Times (30 minutes)

1. Sunday, July 15, immediately following worship, Parlor
2. Wednesday, July 18, 5:45 P.M., Fellowship Hall

Council members will contact assigned names from the new-member list and invite them to attend. The phone conversation to enlist them might go as follows:

"Hello. This is [name]. I am a member of the University Heights Church Council, and we are asking some of those who have joined the church in the past five years to be a part of a focus group discussion. Our outreach consultants, Bob Perry and Marilyn Nelson, will be leading these discussions."

For Sunday Session:

"Would you be able to stay after worship on Sunday, July 15, for about 30 minutes? It will be helpful to hear from you as we think about the future of our church. Do you think you can make it?"

For Wednesday Session:

"Are you available to take part in a focus-group discussion to be held Wednesday evening? We will meet over dinner in the fellowship hall. Because you are a more recent member, it will be helpful for us to hear from you as we think about the future of our church. Do you think you can make it?"

If the answer is yes, thank the person and record the names to indicate they will be attending. If the answer is no, thank the person and continue with your calling list until the needed slots are filled for the focus group.

Storytelling Exercises

An interesting way to get information about a congregation is to encourage members to tell stories about the history of the congregation. This storytelling can be done at a town-hall meeting of members, or with existing groups of members who regularly meet together (for example, members of the diaconate, elders, church council, and so forth).

A number of storytelling exercises for such meetings are contained in the *Manual for Values-based Tactical Planning*, published and distributed by Organizational Health Associates.[3] When my coauthors of that planning manual and I were designing the values-based process, we discovered that the stories people tell contained surprisingly significant information. Their memories of church life are revealing, and the stories that are passed down as legends are highly meaningful. For instance, one congregation lost its building to fire in the early years of its existence. The stories of heroic members helping the pastor save his books and sermon files expressed the core values of the congregation.

In an article in the *Journal of the American Society for Church Growth*, Tom Steffen suggested eight types of stories that a researcher would be interested in collecting. The eight types are:

1. celebrations: stories about baptisms, weddings, funerals, communion, or holiday meetings
2. charismatic stories: stories about ministry, evangelism, Bible study, or mission trips
3. chastisement: accounts of church discipline or punishment of misbehavior
4. comedic: humorous things that happened at church, church outings, or socials
5. commemorative: church anniversaries, dedications, or mortgage-burnings
6. conflict: stories of congregational conflict over budget, theology, or control
7. courage: recollections of how people dealt with death, illness, or suffering
8. crisis: stories about accidents or financial problems[4]

I would add one category of stories to Steffen's list. With apologies that it is not alliterated like the first eight, I think the list should include:

9.   secrets: stories that reveal the shameful, embarrassing, or traumatic incidents in the congregation's history that people ordinarily do not discuss.

I believe that the flushing out and sharing of the "family secrets" is often essential for the congregation to become healthy and move toward healthy growth. Family-systems theory, pioneered by Murray Bowen, emphasizes how negative and destructive secrecy can be in any human system.

In the telling of these stories, congregation members will reveal a great deal about the strengths of the congregation. The listener must be attuned to sense the emotions being expressed, as well as carefully hearing the words spoken. Interpreting the stories is a very intuitive process, and very often one must decode the meanings of symbols and analogies. Because this is so subjective, those involved should check their interpretations with others who can help correct or balance their opinions. A collaborative process in this interpreting of soft data can help guard against the insertion of personal bias.

Personal Interviews

The most obvious and natural way to gather soft data about a congregation and its perceived strengths is personal interviews, which may be done individually or in small groups. The interviews may be set up formally, or they may be done rather informally in the course of interacting with congregation members. As with focus groups, the interviewer should work with a group of congregation leaders to develop a carefully planned and well-worded set of potential questions. In a focus group, the questions would be asked specifically, perhaps even read verbatim from notes. In interviews, the planned questions would be stated more casually and conversationally. There is a more dialogical format for the interviews.

The questions or issues raised by the interviewer should be designed to help identify the strengths of the congregation, which might include:

1. What most appealed to you and led you to join this congregation?
2. Have you found your first impressions of the congregation's strengths to be accurate?
3. What have you discovered about the congregation that you did not realize when you joined?

How would you complete the following sentences?

1. The thing I like best about this congregation is . . .
2. The thing I think this congregation does better than other congregations is . . .
3. The thing this congregation is most known and respected for is . . .
4. The time I was most proud to be a member of this congregation was . . .
5. When I invite friends to this congregation I tell them they will like . . .
6. I think the strongest program of this congregation is . . .
7. The thing in this congregation that gives me the greatest hope for the future is . . .

Personal interviews, when they are conducted formally, may involve the interviewer taking notes or tape recording the meeting. This can be a distraction for the interviewer and a concern for the interviewee, but it is important to accurately record the results of the interview. When interviews are conducted informally, there should be no recording and probably no taking of notes, unless it can be done very discreetly. It may be feasible to scribble a few words on the back of a paper napkin if it appears to be nothing more than doodling. For the informal interview, the interviewer should make notes as soon as possible after the interview is completed. These notes may include not just the content of the words that were said, but the intuitive impressions taken from the encounter. Listening to soft data input is both a cognitive process and an affective process.

Some combination of the methodologies mentioned in this chapter can provide congregational leaders or consultants with a good understanding of the strengths of a congregation. One must keep in mind, however, that these are the strengths as perceived by the members. Members of the congregation probably have a bias in the congregation's favor. They may not be totally honest with the interviewer, or even with themselves, in their assessment of the congregation's strengths. This may be even truer for the congregation's paid staff. Those who are involved in paid leadership for the congregation have a great deal of their own ego invested in believing that the congregation is doing well.

A common perception of congregation members is, "Our congregation is a friendly congregation." Sometimes that perception on the part of members is accurate in that the people who have been in the congregation for many years know each other well, love each other a great deal, and express that love very openly. That friendliness, however, may not be expressed as well to outsiders. Inside data gathering must be balanced with some outside data gathering in order to secure accurate and verified assessments of the congregation's true strengths.

The person conducting these inside interviews should be someone who is viewed as objective and trustworthy in discussing opinions about the congregation. This means that congregational leaders, clergy, or laity will not be the ideal persons for doing the interviewing. An outside party may be enlisted to conduct interviews, or there may be qualified members of the congregation who do not have great visibility as congregational leaders. These persons may be able to secure responses that are less influenced by interviewees trying to say what they believe the interviewers want to hear.

There are ways in which a congregation can build on the strengths it discovers through self-examination. The next chapter will explore how strength can be built on internal strength; then, in chapter 4, the gathering and evaluating of externally gathered data will be discussed.

3

How Can We Use Our Muscle
to Build More Muscle?

A congregation that understands its unique strengths and assets will be better prepared to conduct ministry and outreach in its community. It is important for congregations, like individuals, to be self-differentiated. It is a major element of identity and self-esteem to know thyself. In *The Purpose Driven Church*, the Rev. Rick Warren noted, "I believe that the most effective evangelistic strategy is to first try to reach those with whom you already have something in common."[1]

Unfortunately, when leaders speak of making specific efforts to evangelize or minister to the needs of certain kinds of people, it is sometimes interpreted as a preference for some people to the exclusion of others. This is not the intent when ministry efforts are focused toward specific people. Warren said, "Jesus targeted his ministry in order to be effective, not to be exclusive."[2] Let it be clear that this author is not, in any way, suggesting that anyone should be excluded from the compassionate ministry and outreach of a congregation. No one is turned away. It is also clear, however, that the greatest opportunities to reach people may naturally come as congregations meet and serve persons who are demographically similar to those who make up the present congregational membership.

Marketing professionals speak of market positioning. One of the questions often asked of businesses by marketing consultants is, "What position do you hold in the market?" By that they are asking whether the business is number one, number two, or way down the list in terms of their effectiveness within their market environment. If there are areas of the market in which an organization is number one, that area of strength may be a primary opportunity for future growth. In other words, that organization may be able to build on its strength.[3]

It is worthwhile for congregational leaders to examine the market position of their congregation in various areas of their work. They might

37

ask themselves, "In terms of public relations and a positive community image, is our congregation number one, number two, number three, and so forth?" This self-evaluation could apply to dozens of areas of congregational life, including:

- quality of music programs
- inspirational value of worship
- location and visibility of facilities
- friendliness of the people
- effectiveness of children's and youth programs
- safety and attractiveness of infant care facilities
- effectiveness of congregational ministries to community social needs

When a congregation identifies areas where its market position is number one or two in a community, that may indicate an area of strength that can be built upon. There will likely be creative ways to extend and broaden those areas of already effective work.

One aspect of market positioning is determining the public's perception of how well a given congregation is doing in an area of endeavor. This is one of those places where perception tends to become reality. When congregational leaders evaluate the market position of their congregation, they will do well to ask themselves, "Is this number-one rating we have in our market based on current reality, or may it be a perception left from an earlier day or a different circumstance?" Sometimes what is perceived as a congregational strength may be a mirage.

Congregations can improve their market position in several ways:

1. Improve an area of congregational life, and publicize that improvement widely.
2. Encourage congregation members to speak often and glowingly of a specific strength of the congregation. This is the "word of mouth" public relations and can be priceless.
3. Study and learn from the market leaders, and find the transferable principles in what they are doing that will apply to your context.
4. Search for aspects of congregational strength that are truly unique to your fellowship. Those uniquenesses are a prime opportunity for a leading position in a market.

In *Managing for Results*, Peter Drucker, one of the great organizational thinkers of our time, noted that in the 1960s the railroads decided that they were weak in the area of short-haul transportation of people and goods. They could not compete with cars, trucks, and buses for short-trip carrying. At that point, the railroads decided to concentrate their marketing on long hauls, the area where they had greater strength and could be more competitive.[4] This is a good example of how an organization can assess its strength and strategize to develop its future based on these areas of strength.

Communities of faith can do the same. Here are some examples of how a congregation might build on its strengths.

Temple Beth Israel

Temple Beth Israel was small, but they had an unusually large number of attorneys who were members of the congregation. They discovered that within their congregation and their community, there were many senior adults who were comfortably middle-class, and who had neglected matters of estate planning. Among those outside the congregation in this category, a survey revealed that the people realized they needed to work on this matter of importance to individuals and families, but they found it an area where it was easy to procrastinate. Beth Israel decided that they could offer their own members and people in the community the services of some of their attorney members. They developed the following list of potential projects:

- free estate-planning seminars
- simple will-writing services
- personal counsel with those needing legal advice about matters of estate planning
- assistance with tax-advantageous ways of giving to charitable and religious causes
- occasional newsletter articles or bulletin inserts to inform people about related issues or changes in law
- the formation of an endowment fund for the congregation
- referral services to appropriate resources for those needing specialized assistance

Beth Israel took a strength of their congregation and translated it into potential ministry and outreach.

Main Street Church

Main Street Church, located in a small county-seat town, had a number of persons who were artists, including the pastor. Among them were people who painted, some with oils or acrylics, some with watercolors. Others in the congregation designed stained-glass windows. A few worked with pottery and ceramics. One man did large sculpture projects as an avocation. The pastor called these members together to brainstorm ways they could use their talent and passion for art as a blessing for the work of the congregation. They developed several ideas for potential ministries, including:

- maintaining art displays in the halls and gathering places of the church
- hosting art exhibits at the church several times a year
- holding special season exhibits open to the public (Christmas nativities, Easter art, etc.)
- offering art classes for young people and for retirees
- helping with better use of religious art in the worship center and in worship services
- offering art displays or speakers to local schools
- providing art appreciation events and experiences for preschool children

Bethlehem Church

Bethlehem Church had five doctors and seven nurses who were members. They utilized this strength to help these medical professionals provide a free clinic for persons in poverty, a well-baby clinic, and health screening for senior adults. They also formed a Parish Nursing ministry with people prepared to assist individuals with specific nursing needs and to respond to any emergencies that might arise at church activities. They discovered a need in the community for health consultation and follow-up for persons recovering from cardiac surgery. They began a task force to address this need.

Christ Church

Christ Church became aware that it had a wealth of members who had experience in the building trades. Among them were two retired contractors, an architect, three plumbers, and two electricians. In addition, there were several dozen men and women who had experience with do-it-yourself home repair and remodeling. After mobilizing and blessing this group as a Christian Builders Ministry, the church saw these people:

- build two houses with Habitat for Humanity
- provide minor repair and winterizing services for senior adults in the community
- re-roof seven homes for underprivileged families
- build a room addition on a home for a family that had a set of triplets
- rebuild for a family that had fire damage to their home
- paint five houses as a part of a community improvement project

In addition, the group went on mission trips to construct a church building in Honduras, a medical clinic in Mexico, and a seminary library in Liberia.

Much of what has been mentioned above is already happening in many congregations, including those that are small and midsize. Sadly, sometimes the real impact of the ministry involved is not as well known and as appreciated as would be desired. In some cases, the ministries have great outreach potential, but the element of evangelism and witness in the project is neglected or mishandled. This is a reminder of the importance of strategy and intentionality in all ministry and outreach efforts of the congregation. People are to be served, but it is vital that they also have an opportunity to understand that the motive behind that ministry is to express God's love for them.

One of the essential elements to beginning creative ministries built on the unique strengths of a congregation is to remember the experimental nature of such ventures. A ministry experiment means that there may be as much prospect for failure as there is for success. There is a continuum of congregational attitudes toward new ideas and approaches that runs from being rigid, traditional, and permission-withholding at one end, and very adventurous, open, and permission-giving at the other. Congregations fall somewhere on that continuum in their general outlook toward new initiatives. Permission-giving congregations allow leaders to try new things, and they affirm the effort even when it does not achieve the desired result.

Don't Hide Your Edsel

In *Innovation and Entrepreneurship: Practice and Principles*, Drucker told the story of the Edsel. In the 1950s, Ford Motor Company realized that it did not have a car in the upper-middle market to compete with the Buicks and Oldsmobiles made by General Motors. Their design teams went to work and came up with the ill-fated Edsel. After the dismal failure of the Edsel to sell, Ford did not drop the subject. They had investigators do an in-depth study of why it had not worked. The investigators learned that the tastes of their upper-middle class market were changing. Out of that research, Ford redesigned another model it had recently introduced, the Thunderbird. The Thunderbird became the greatest success of any car since Henry Ford introduced the Model T in 1908.[5]

The Thunderbird became so successful that in today's retro trend in car design, the Thunderbird is being reintroduced with many of the same charming lines of the original. All this from a failure.

A major aspect of market-driven planning is the willingness to experiment. Building new ministries on congregational strengths can go wrong. Sometimes congregations will discover that what they thought was a strength was not as strong as they had hoped. Sometimes the group may indeed have a strength, but may lack anyone with the passion to turn it into ministry. (The fact you have doctors in the congregation does not mean that a clinic ministry is going to work.) Experimental ministries can fail for lack of good leadership. They may not work due to the wrong timing for their launch. There are many ways to fail, but the task following the project is always the same: learn. The lessons learned may be painful to process, but the learning may result in tremendous success and effectiveness in days to come. Remember that the Edsel was an essential step in getting to the Thunderbird.

Through the inside data gathering discussed in chapter 2, a congregation can become more aware of what its members perceive to be its greatest strengths. The interviewing includes questions that search for that information, both directly and indirectly. The direct question might be, "What do you find to be the unique strengths of this congregation." An indirect question might be worded, "When you invite friends to visit this congregation, what do you mention as a reason they might enjoy it? The analysis of the responses to questions like these provides an initial understanding of congregational strengths.

Internal Research in Pilot Project Church

My wife Marilyn Nelson and I conducted a pilot project at University Heights Baptist Church. Our goal was to test whether studying congregational strengths actually helped a congregation develop better methods of outreach. In working with the congregational leaders at UHBC, we decided to identify not only the strengths of the congregation, but to supplement these strengths with an analysis of congregational core values. These core values are the attitudes and beliefs that members say are essential and define the congregation. They help identify what is the passion and driving force of congregational life. Portions of the final report of the consultants are included here so that the reader may get an overall picture of the final product produced by this planning process. UHBC leaders were told that items listed in the report were suggestions for church consideration. We expected that church leaders would need to add other information as they studied the report. Some items would need to be deleted or amended in order to be most useful and relevant to the church.

The report began with a section called, "Who Are We?" University Heights Baptist Church is a healthy, midsize Baptist church affiliated with the American Baptist Churches and the Cooperative Baptist Fellowship. Locally it cooperates with the Missouri Baptist Convention and the Greene County Baptist Association.

UHBC manifests the following core values: integrity, active caring, worship, freedom, diversity of thought, learning, authentic witness, and missions. These core values are descriptive of the church, and they also serve as a compass for keeping the church on track as it envisions its future.

- Integrity: UHBC values honesty and ethical conduct in all aspects of church ministry and Christian living.
- Active caring: UHBC values hands-on, practical assistance offered to church members and nonmembers who have needs (not just talk, but incarnated care).

- Worship: UHBC values meaningful, inspirational worship that has variety, but respects the traditions of Christian worship.
- Freedom: UHBC values soul freedom in Christ and all of its related concepts: priesthood of the believer, autonomy of the local congregation and religious freedom (church/state separation).
- Diversity of thought: UHBC values the differences of opinion and interpretation that result when Christians join together around the essential common elements of faith, but members may disagree on matters of less important detail.
- Learning: UHBC values education and lifelong learning, especially as related to spiritual growth and the development of maturity in Christ.
- Authentic witness: UHBC values evangelism that is true to the Gospel, ethical and non-manipulative in its application, and lovingly relational in its methodology.
- Mission: UHBC values the entire enterprise of world missions, and gives time, money, and energy to supporting missionaries globally. UHBC further encourages its members to be on mission and provides them with opportunities to personally engage in mission activities.

UHBC has the following strengths: excellent music, meaningful traditional worship, sincere welcoming, high education level, care for one another, willing volunteerism, progressive thinking, generosity, children's ministry, and effective leadership.

UHBC is *the* place in southwest Missouri for traditional moderate Baptists, Baptists who value equal service opportunities for women, and Baptists who support the American Baptist Churches (ABC) or the Cooperative Baptist Fellowship (CBF). This would include new Southwest Missouri State University students and faculty coming from ABC or moderate Southern Baptist Convention churches, and people looking for an authentic faith expression without reference to denominational labels.

The church is unique in its dual alignment with multiple Baptist conventions, and it has a history of valuing that diversity of denominational involvement. The church has a strong history of missions support. There has been long-term, stable pastoral leadership, and the church is the strongest it has been in its history.

The second section of the consultants' report contained suggestions for future action that had been developed by the consultants and church leaders. The healthy congregation builds on its strengths and at the same time attempts to gain strength in areas of weakness. In order to build on strengths, the following things were suggested:

1. Emphasize and promote awareness of the core values, both within the congregation and with outreach materials. This identifies who UHBC is. It helps people know whether they will find their place at UHBC. This can be done through a series of sermons by the pastor on each of the core values, printing the values on the bulletin, brochures, newsletters, and other publications, and on the church Web site.

2. Monitor to see that church budgeting, scheduling, and staffing are consistent with the values. For example, if excellent music is a value, the church should protect scheduling so that conflicts do not diminish the ability of the choirs and other music programs to rehearse and plan, and the congregation should budget adequately for quality musicians and musical presentations. If the congregation values sincere welcoming, constant efforts should be made to make the church more visitor-friendly and convenient for newcomers. Since worship is a value for the church, worship should be carefully coordinated each week with representatives of preaching, music, drama, and gifted laypersons planning for the themes of each worship service to be enhanced by all elements of the service.

3. In the welcoming of visitors, the consultants suggest that the church make the following changes:
    a. In asking attendees to sign the register, avoid the negative idea of saying, "We won't use the information to harass you." Most people will not assume they will be harassed by the church, and the denial of that intention seems defensive.
    b. Have the registers sent down the aisle and signed, then sent back to the place of origin so that people can see the names of those with whom they are sitting, and members can note whether others on the register are visitors. Explain this procedure each Sunday and encourage members to make use of this way of getting acquainted with newcomers (and members they may not know).
    c. The Sunday school greeters do a great job, but there may be a need to have similar greeting and information services available for those who come late or just for the worship service.

d. Church signage should include helpful diagrams of the layout of the buildings and the times of activities posted at two or three key points of entry or circulation. There might also be a couple of posters with pictures to help newcomers identify the members of the ministry staff. Additionally, the signage might be improved to help newcomers know where to enter the building and where to find the welcome and information center.

The strengthening of areas of weakness for University Heights is difficult for the consultants to address. The church does not have any glaring weaknesses that were immediately observable. It is an exceptionally blessed and effective congregation. The one area of church life that we believe should be given increased emphasis is evangelism and outreach. The church has been fortunate to have a number of well-trained, mature leaders transfer from other Baptist churches in recent years. The effectiveness of the church in reaching new converts or previously unchurched persons has not been as strong as their appeal to Baptists and other Christians who have transferred to UHBC from other congregations. This project is an effort in that direction, but the church will need to continue to search for ways to mobilize members in effective witnessing and faith sharing.

What Niches Should the Church Consider Attempting to Reach?

Based on all of the research and observations that have been done, it appears that there are several market niches that would be possible outreach or ministry focuses for UHBC. The internal studies of congregational strengths and values, and the external data gathered, lead us to suggest the following eight possibilities for discussion by church leaders.

1. Well-educated and fairly affluent adults in their 50s and 60s who live in suburbs east and south of the location of the church. This is primarily in zip codes 65804, 65807, and 65809.
2. Moderate Baptists and other evangelicals who are related to the University communities of Springfield.
3. Musicians and others who appreciate the fine arts.
4. Incoming corporate management personnel new to Springfield.

5. Young couples and families with small children.
6. Parents of youth who want for them a personalized, high-quality, spiritual development experience rather than a large, flashy youth program.
7. International students.
8. Single mothers who live within five miles of the church (if a member or members of the church indicate a passion for engaging in such a ministry).

It was understood that UHBC would attempt to address some but not all of these potential niche groups. The next section of the consultants' report had specific suggestions for strategizing to reach certain of these niches. That material is found in chapter 5, where strategies are discussed.

A Sample Agenda

As the consultants began to meet with the UHBC council, the leaders of major programs of the church, and the chairpersons of standing committees, the meetings were conducted with the guidance of an agenda that included elements such as the following:

- Get acquainted.
- Explain the process for the summer; outline elements of the internal study (Who we are and what we do well), and the external study (Who is out there and what are their needs?).
- Discuss Core Values of UHBC—discuss and amend these possible core values, which were identified based on the facilitators' conversations with the pastor: Integrity, active caring, worship, freedom, diversity of thought, learning, authentic witness
- A Discussion Exercise: The Church of Today and the Church of Tomorrow—offer words that describe this church as it is today and then what the congregation might be five years from now. Record the responses on a marker board, and discuss the changes and challenges involved in moving the congregation from current reality to future dream.
- Schedule the next meeting (possibly additional meetings at two-week intervals)
- Assignments for teams (sub-groups) to complete by the next meeting:
    Team One: Observation of how visitor-friendly the church is. Attend the next few Sundays, attempting to experience the church as if you

were a first-time visitor. Observe everything you can about finding the church, knowing service times, finding parking, knowing where to go in, how you are welcomed, how friendly people are toward outsiders, and so forth. Take notes and prepare suggestions for improvement. (These observations will be considered along with those made by the outside consultants in their initial visits.)

Team Two: Secure a list of names, addresses, and phone numbers of persons who have joined the church in the past five years. Work with Bob and Marilyn toward setting up a focus-group meeting for interviewing a group of at least 10 of these persons.

Team Three: Prepare a pin map to locate the home addresses of those who have joined the church in the past five years. Use two colors of markers: one for new members by transfer, another for new members by baptism.

Team Four: What do secular advertisers know that we need to know? Identify major highways with billboards within 10 miles of the church. Drive the highway and have a passenger note the subject, color scheme, basis of appeal, and apparent target age group of the billboards. Note impressions of what is being advertised and how it is being sold.

- Questions, comments, unresolved concerns
- Prayer for God's guidance and wisdom; adjourn

As the niche marketing group at UHBC worked together in its first meeting, the conversation was lively and engaging. The council affirmed the core values as being accurate and only amended the list by adding one more value at UHBC: missions. The congregation is involved in missions at all levels, including many hands-on partnership projects in Springfield and other places.

The group developed the following lists of words to describe the congregation at that time and as they envisioned it five years in the future.

UHBC Today
- Diverse
- Unique
- Accepting
- Flexible

- Prayer
- Caring family
- Service opportunities
- Listening
- Excellent music
- Active
- Volunteerism
- Forward thinking
- Sincerely welcoming
- Conservative (holding historic Baptist values)

UHBC 5 Years from Today

- Hope to be more widely known
- Have more families with elementary-age children
- Let the church be known as a place of acceptance of diverse opinions
- Correct false impressions some may have of UHBC
- Better promo of fine musical presentations
- More events packed out like Christmas Eve
- Childcare services offered
- More parking space
- More singles; more ministry to single parents
- Every member involved in mission service
- Double our present attendance; provide more lists of people to be visited

Council Members were asked to volunteer for one of the research teams that fit their interest or expertise. They agreed to form the following teams to report at the next meeting:

Team 1	Guest-friendly observation	Ken and Jim
Team 2	Name/addresses for new members	Charlene and Lois
Team 3	Pin map of recent members	Ted and Todd
Team 4	Billboard observation	Pat, Lois, & Michael

Table 3.1   Research Teams and Leaders

Name	Age by Decade	Years Member	Miles from Church
Gary & Brenda H.	50s & 60s	2-1/2	8
Phil & Norma J.	50s & 60s	2-1/2	5
Michael P.	20s	0	10
Ed & Janice	60s	5	1
Joby & Vickie W.	30s	1	10
Jeannie & Bill G.	50s & 60s	1	5
Ron & Alice W.	30s & 50s	2	35
Dan and Joe B.	60s	2	10

Table 3.2   Inside Focus Group Participants

Any congregation can build on its areas of effectiveness and greater resources. With those strengths as a base of operation, the congregation can stretch itself by launching into new areas of ministry. The next task to address is the locating of persons with needs who are not being adequately served through social services, governmental assistance, and faith-based ministries systems. These niche groups are out there waiting for someone to express care and concern for them.

Report on Inside Focus Group Participants

What most appealed to you about UHBC and led you to join this church?

- The warmth and friendliness from everyone—not just certain groups.
- Michael—a wonderful pastor.
- Gorgeous building—beautiful stained-glass windows.
- Music in worship services.
- Diversity—the inclusion of women in key roles.
- Friendliness of Sunday school class.
- The positive message the church gives to its members—a consistent message—nuturing after you are members.
- Radio message the pastor had—not preaching, but conversing.
- The program called "A Month of Sundays," which allowed community members to visit churches in the city. A couple that visited was warmly received and able to meet the pastor—very impressed.
- Sense of tolerance and acceptance in the church—much more than other churches.
- No compromise of essential faith and principles.
- The church cares for its children—community feeling—everyone cares about our child.
- The traditional style of the worship services.
- Friendliness from the first visit—the pastor and everyone.
- Sermons that are intellectually challenging.

What have you discovered about the church that you did not realize when you joined?

- I found here what I needed even though I didn't realize the need when I joined.
- I felt the church would be open to including women and found that it was.
- I learned after being a member for a while that it is a good church, but not perfect.
- Very educational. There is the opportunity to hear other points of view.
- Open Sunday school—you can select the class that suits you.

If you could change one thing about the church, what would it be?

Open Sunday school—you can select the class that suits you.
- Have more classes on marriage, parenting, and relationships.
- Add classes on how to parent God's way—perhaps use a video series.
- Improve scheduling of church programs and meetings—sometimes important activities are scheduled at the same time.

4

Where Are the Lost Fragments?

Many of the same techniques utilized for internal evaluation of the congregation can be used to gather relevant data from outside the congregation—to verify and supplement that insider information. A congregation's self-concept may be skewed, and a truer and fuller picture is needed. External research can also be used in the development of a market-driven plan for church outreach and ministry to gain a clearer understanding of the context in which ministry is to be done. It is an effort to read the context.

Market-driven planning specifically involves identifying those persons in difficult circumstances whose needs are being overlooked. They fall through the cracks of congregational programming, and often are not served well by government and private helping programs. In many cases, their needs have spiritual elements that only the faith community can adequately address. The task for the congregation is to read the community, to get to know the people who live there, and to identify ways to serve them.

Among the characteristics being explored are the unmet needs of people in the broader community. In *Segmentation Marketing*, John Berrigan and Carl Finkbeiner explain, "Customer needs are the basis of a market-driven approach. Needs are internal, and they are the factors that determine the choices that people make."[1] Abraham Maslow, a social theorist, provides a helpful model for thinking about the variety of needs people have. Maslow developed a pyramid of needs he believed motivate people. Depending on their context, people may tend to be at differing points in their placement in this hierarchy of needs. At the lower end of the pyramid were basic physical and survival needs, and toward the higher end were needs for relationship, belonging, and self-fulfillment. Maslow noted that persons might at given times in their lives be at various points in these levels of needs. Applying Maslow's hierarchy to niche ministry planning, it has been observed that in lower socioeconomic settings, the meeting of needs such as basic survival requirements may be the way to build relationships. In higher socioeconomic settings, most of the basic needs may be met due to the affluence of the constituency, so the points of contact may be more related to issues of actualization, or finding meaning in life. In order to understand fully the needs of your community's residents, you want to discover their lower-level needs but also their higher-level interests, values, and desires.

External Assessment Techniques

Among the choices for research methods mentioned in chapter 2 is the contrasting pair of quantitative and qualitative research. Quantitative data is more statistical, objective, and precise. Qualitative research requires good skills of observation, intuitive analysis, and the interpretation of feelings.

Another pair of research approaches, particularly in the design of survey questions, is the choice between open-ended and closed-ended questions. Closed-ended questions are written in such a way that they require short answers, often yes or no. An example of a closed-ended question would be, "Have you ever worn shorts to a worship service of the congregation?" The question calls for an answer of yes or no. In fact, the instructions on the questionnaire may say for the respondent to answer with yes or no, true or false, or never or always.

Open-ended questions tend to be what schoolteachers have called essay questions. They do not call for a short answer, and they may encourage the respondent to express considerable philosophy or rationale in the expression of the answer. An example of an open-ended question would be, "Statistics show that many people who went to church as children drop out of church during their late teens or twenties. Why do you think this is so?" This style of question encourages people to speak or write at length, and it can result in information far beyond the issue stated. It may reveal much about the attitudes, beliefs, and assumptions of the respondent.

Another way of approaching sociological research is by utilizing both direct and indirect methods. Direct research involves personal contact with the subjects of the research. Methods such as interviewing, focus groups, mall intercepts, and surveys are considered direct research because the researcher is in direct contact with the people being studied. Indirect research includes such methods as studying demographics, marketing research reports, and public records. There is no personal contact with the subjects of the research.

It should be noted that these research approaches often overlap. Qualitative research may be done using either direct or indirect approaches, and either open- or close-ended questions. Quantitative research will usually involve more close-ended questions in order to have statistical data for compilation and analysis. It is up to researchers, however, to decide what provides the best mix of approaches for any given research project.

Among the major resources or techniques that are useful in doing external research are the demographic data, outside focus groups, mall intercepts, written questionnaires, man-on-the-street interviews, observations, and Web-based research.

Demographic Data

There are many sources for demographic data, but most of the basic information is derived from the U.S. Census Bureau, which is conducted every 10 years. Various marketing and demographic research companies take the census data and organize it to reveal lifestyle and marketing information. In some cases they supplement the census data with additional research that they conduct to provide more specific and specialized information. There may be costs involved in securing the professionally organized data, but the basic information is available free from the census bureau.

Some of the Web sites that will be of interest to persons securing demographic information include:

*   **www.census.gov.** This site accesses the U.S. Census Bureau. It provides information from the most recent census, and reports can be written according to zip codes or census tracts. There are maps available and various ways of customizing the reports to provide the information desired. The census data reports include information about a given population in terms of age range, education level, ethnic background, marital status, housing, and many other details. There is no charge for the data downloaded from the census bureau site.

- **www.demographics.caci.com.** CACI is a marketing information company. Their site provides information about their services, and they offer a free zip code sample report that has a summary of data for a requested zip code.
- **www.claritas.com.** Claritas combines census data, U.S. Bureau of Labor statistics, and newspaper reports. They utilize the PRIZM system of organizing the population into lifestyle clusters of persons who share common demographic characteristics.
- **www.scanus.com.** This company organizes data from government and other sources to identify lifestyle marketing information. Their reports can be secured based on zip codes, census tracts, or specified distance radii around an address point. Customized reports can be requested in relation to areas drawn based on highways, rivers, county lines, or other boundaries designated by the purchaser.
- **www.percept.com.** Percept goes beyond the above organizations by including the faith element in their data. They explore the areas of church attendance patterns, attitudes toward church and religion, and openness to increased church involvement. They also indicate whether the preferences of people in the studied area would tend toward traditional or contemporary expressions of faith. Percept also offers an inexpensive summary report.
- **www.visions-decisions.com.** This organization prepares demographic and general studies for congregations, judicatories, and denominations. Anthony Healy is president of Visions-Decisions, Inc., and their offices are located in Atlanta.

Many regional denominational bodies have contracts with marketing companies to provide information to member churches at a discounted rate or at no cost. A church should inquire of their local district, association, diocese, or conference about whether such a contract is in place. This will make the ordering of professional marketing reports either free or at greatly discounted prices.

Analyzing demographic data to find meaningful market information is the next task. The census information includes: numbers of persons in a given area broken down by age bracket, family situation, vehicles per household, home ownership, race, educational level, and income level. The marketing company reports provide additional information and have various ways of classifying groups of people by lifestyle, buying power, product preferences, and so forth.

Comparing the data of persons in the study area with the national average is a helpful tool. For example, in one area studied for this book, the average age of residents was 41.1 years of age, and the U.S. national average age is 36.6. This tells you that you are looking at a local population that includes many more older adults than the average or typical U.S. community. The same area has 33 percent of the adult population with college degrees, whereas the national average is 20 percent.

The demographic data may reveal various kinds of potential niche groups for ministry or congregational outreach. Some of the possibilities include:

1. elderly persons living alone
2. persons in households with no vehicle
3. male single-parent families
4. female single-parent families
5. single persons of various age groups
6. racial groups
7. persons living in multifamily housing
8. college students
9. low-income families
10. families with preschool children (and other age brackets)
11. persons living in an area of high unemployment

A primary value in a congregation studying local demographics is to discover the needs that people in the community may feel. These needs may include things that are practical (e.g., childcare, social relationships, or parenting assistance), emotional (e.g., relationships or self-esteem), or spiritual (e.g., exploration of life meaning, need to connect with God, or concern about death and eternity). It is also interesting to note whether the demographic makeup of the community is very different from the demographic profile of the church. Over time this often happens. Many congregations that began as "neighborhood" congregations have seen their members move away from the immediate area in which they are located, and their membership demographic may be very different from that of the local community. One pastor who did this analysis as a part of a Doctor of Ministry degree confirmed what is true for many congregations, that the community resident profile around the church was significantly different from that of the church member profile. Church members in this congregation tended to be much older, with a much more traditional family structure and were much more economically affluent than the people who lived around the church.[2] Discovering such differences between community and congregation can help ministry planners understand why the congregation has difficulty connecting with its immediate community.

Table 4.1 below shows some examples of demographic analyses based on the project conducted at University Heights Baptist Church:

There are some noteworthy elements in the vrious zip code statistics in the report done for University Heights Church:

- 65806—The percentage of single parent families in the population is 35 percent compared to a national average of 21 percent. This means that the number in that zip code is 37 percent more than the national

---

Zip codes identified as the church's area of influence:

    65804—from church south to co. line, west to 65
    65802—mostly west of downtown
    65803—north of town
    65806—north Springfield
    65807—south Springfield
    65809—east of town
    65810—southwest of town

Category	65804	65802	65803	65806	65807	65809	65810	Total
Population	36,000	36,000	37,000	10,000	49,000	8,000	13,000	189,000
Non-anglo %	4%	3%	2.3%	10%	7%	3%	8%	4.6% avg.
Age difference from U.S. average	+5	0	0	-3	0	+3	-1	n/a
Income difference from U.S. average	+17K	-19K	-20K	-45K	-8K	+82K	+32K	+5.6K
Single parent homes difference from U.S. average	-6%	+4%	-6%	-6%	-6%	-6%	-6%	-6%
College Graduate difference from U.S. average:	+13%	+4%	0	37%	-4%	-16%	-15%	+1%

Table 4.1 Sample Demographic Summary Based on University Heights Baptist Church

average. This zip code has a family income level that is $45,000 below the US national average family income. This would appear to be a niche the congregation should consider developing ministries to serve. There are needs present in this group that a church like UHBC could address.

- 65807—This appears to be a very middle-income, middle-class, average American community.
- 65809—The population growth from 1980 to 1990 (based on other data consulted) was 33 percent compared to a national average of 10 percent. This area is extremely affluent and of an extremely high educational level.
- 65810—Supplementary data indicated that the population growth from 1980 to 1990 was 37 percent compared to national average of 10 percent. The growth for 1990 to 2000 was 47 percent compared to 10 percent nationally. This area is also considerably more economically affluent that the national average.
- Scan U.S. provides lifestyle cluster information based on its PRIZM system of grouping persons according to socioeconomic, educational, and other lifestyle characteristics. See table 4.2.

Psychographic and Marketing Information

Psychographic analysis of a community involves going beyond the raw census information to attempt to understand the basic values, beliefs, and lifestyles of people. It is an effort to discover what motivates them and what are the deeper issues of life for them. This kind of information is helpful for companies attempting to sell a product or service. Author Sarah White says, "Psychographic research studies the activities, interest and opinions of the individuals who make up the market."[3] It deals with the "why" of what people do or decide. Congregations, to even a greater extent than commercial enterprises, can benefit from understanding these deeper motivations. When you are exploring these areas of life, you are getting closer to the spiritual aspects that are the primary concern of the faith community.

In most cases, reliable psychographic information will need to be purchased, unless it is available by contract through a church judicatory, as mentioned earlier. Sometimes a congregation may have members who are involved in marketing for secular organizations, and who are able to access

Category	Year 2000	2005 proj.
Population	212,600	224,300
25–34 yrs. of age	27,000	25,000
35–44 yrs. of age	35,000	40,000
Average family income	$63,091	$73,708
Single-person households	24,300	26,600
Households with no vehicle	5,700	6,000
Single males with children	952	n/a
Single females with children	4,389 (5.1%)	n/a

Mobility of the population:	20% newcomers (less than year in present home)
	54% have lived in the area less than 5 years
	22% have lived in the area more than 15 years

Summary of Largest PRIZM Lifestyle Clusters in the Study Area

14%	Family Scrabble (blue collar, renter, often hispanic)	U.S. average: 2.3%
13%	Smalltown Downtown (white collar, single parents, young adult)	U.S. average: 1.5%

Table 4.2 SCAN U.S. Summary of Church Area: 5-mile Radius around the Church, UHBC

this kind of information for congregational use. The kind of data helpful to a congregation might be: radio and television outlets preferred by certain kinds of people, sections of the newspaper read most frequently by certain people, or how people in the area feel about various styles of music. This information may assist a congregation in making decisions about worship style and the ways of best investing their advertising and public relations budgets.

Gathering Your Own Data

In addition to relying on information gathered by the U.S. Census Bureau or market research organizations, niche ministry planners can gather their own data using a variety of techniques. The design process is an essential part of research's success, and the value of the data secured will be directly proportional to the quality of the survey instrument. Some of the key questions to ask in the design process are:

1. What are we trying to learn? What specific information do we hope to gain from this effort? What is the key question for which we are seeking an answer?
2. Who should we ask in order to get the most useful information on this subject? How can we locate and contact the persons who can best inform us about this?
3. When is the best time to encounter the group we wish to question? How can we make the timing of our research most effective for finding the information we seek?
4. How can we best phrase the questions? Can we avoid misunderstandings, and can we make the answers easier to evaluate?

A few of the cardinal rules for writing research questions are:

1. Make each question and the entire survey as concise and precise as possible.
2. Avoid using words that are ambiguous or emotionally loaded. In dealing with the public, for example, a word such as *unchurched* may be heard by some as being pejorative, or it may be subject to a wide range of interpretations.

3. Do not ask questions in a way that leads the respondent toward a certain answer. An example of a leading question might be, "Do you think the world would be a better place if everyone had a strong religious faith?" The question seems to be begging for a particular response.
4. Do not use technical or complex language in asking questions.
5. Do not reveal the identity of the organization sponsoring the survey if that is likely to influence how people will answer. (The way people respond to questions about their drinking habits may be influenced by whether the researcher represents Budweiser or Baptists.)
6. Place the questions in a logical order so that they flow from general to specific and less threatening to more revealing.

Outside Focus Groups

Focus groups are a useful tool for planners who want to gather their own psychographic information. In chapter 2, we dealt with the use of inside focus groups to explore the internal strengths of a church. Getting to know the strengths and needs of the community can also be facilitated by forming focus groups of persons outside the church. The key difference in the formation of a focus group of this kind is that the participants generally will have to be compensated. You are asking persons who have no personal interest in the congregation to give their time and share their opinions for the benefit of the church. This payment often takes the form of $40 to $75 per participant in cash or gift certificates. In very affluent areas, this payment may have to be even higher to get the right kinds of people to participate. Generally, a focus group requires at least six, but no more than twelve people, to be effective.

It is risky to draw conclusions based on a single focus group. Multiple focus groups are always desirable in the investigation of a particular issue. Following are samples from a focus group conducted by a new congregation in the research area. While it is preferable to have multiple focus groups for a given project, the difficulty enlisting this group caused the leaders to glean what information it could from the group and depend on other research techniques for additional data.

The Design of the Project

In this case, focus-group planners decided to try to enlist young adults between the ages of 25 and 45 who lived in the area being targeted for RiverSouth, the new church start. They scheduled the meeting for a Wednesday night, hoping that would eliminate some of those persons who were active in evangelical churches that had regular Wednesday night activities. It was important to have some of the focus group be parents of young children, so the planners would screen for that demographic. People could be used if they were not parents, but it was important to know in order to have at least a fair representation of parents. Potential participants were offered $50 to compensate them for the two-hour meeting.

The location for the focus group was based on (1) where the focus group participants lived and (2) the size of the group expected. Refreshments were served. The space was free community space, but some planners will need to rent space. Names of potential participants were chosen at random from a directory of streets and subdivisions in the target area. Those contacted were told only that a group considering opening a new venture in the community needed focus-group feedback. As participants were enlisted, their names, addresses, and phone numbers were written down so that a confirmation letter could be sent to them. The script used for enlisting participants and the letter sent to confirm their attendance are provided on the next page.

Script for Phone Calls
to Enlist Participants in Focus Group

"Hello! My name is Bob Perry, and I am representing a local group putting together a focus group. You will be paid $50 if you participate in the focus group that will meet for two hours on Wednesday, January 26, in the community room at Ukrop's Supermarket across from Chesterfield Town Center. Would you be willing to join us at 6:30 that evening?" (*yes or no*)

- If the response is no, say, "Thank you very much. I won't take any more of your time. Have a good evening."

- If the response is yes, say, "I need to ask you two questions to determine if you fit our focus group requirements. Are you between the ages of 20 and 45 years old?" (*yes or no*)

- If the response is no, say, "I'm sorry, but we need the focus group participants to fit that age bracket. Thank you for your time this evening."

- If the response is yes, proceed to the next question: "Do you have children living at home?" (*yes or no*)

- If the response is no, the person can still qualify as long as a majority of the participants do have children. If the response is yes, say, "Great, you fit the profile. We will meet at 6:30 P.M. on Wednesday, January 26, at the community room at the Ukrop's across from Chesterfield Town Center. We will have light refreshments available, so you may want to arrive a few minutes early. At the meeting we will ask you some opinion questions, but they will not be highly personal or embarrassing. They are designed to help us know how to best advertise and promote a new venture that is considering locating in Chesterfield County. At the close of the two-hour meeting, you will be paid $50. Do you have any questions?"

- Conclude: "Thank you. I will look forward to seeing you on January 26."

Sample Letter to Focus Group Participants

To: Participants in the Marketing Focus Group, January 26

From: Focus Group Facilitators Exploring a New Enterprise in Chesterfield County

Thank you for your willingness to be a part of the focus group. We will meet at the community meeting room at the Ukrop's, across from Chesterfield Town Center. The group will consist of approximately 20 Chesterfield County residents.

You will complete a one-page written survey form; following that, we will allow about 60 to 75 minutes of conversation. The discussion will deal with matters of your preferences and opinions about living in Chesterfield County, your interest in various types of music and entertainment, and other such things.

If you have never been a part of a focus group, you will find this experience both interesting and rewarding; one reward being the $50 you will receive as you leave. Dress for the meeting is informal. Light refreshments will be available.

If you are unable to attend, please call 000-0000. Please make every effort to arrive on time. We hope to begin promptly at 6:30 P.M., so that we can end the session at 8:30 P.M.

We look forward to meeting you Wednesday evening.

Thanks,

Bob Perry

Focus group planners should be aware that setting up such a group can be challenging. The three team members at RiverSouth spent a total of eight hours on the phone trying to enlist participants. They had thought that offering $50 for two hours of evening time would be a useful incentive, but that did not prove to be the case. They made approximately 240 dialups, and completed about 85 calls to enlist 11 persons to attend. On the original date of the meeting, there was a severe ice storm in Richmond, and all public events had to be postponed. The leaders again contacted everyone who was scheduled to come, and they sent another letter with the information for the new meeting time. One person called to cancel the morning of the event, and five failed to show up. This meant that a more efficient and effective means of enlisting participants was needed for future group formation.

A possible conclusion drawn from the difficulty in enlisting persons to exchange two hours of their time for $50 in cash is that time is a currency of higher value than money for many of the residents of Chesterfied County. As RiverSouth leaders plan outreach and ministry efforts, they would be wise to remind themselves that their customers will not be patient with any perceived time-wasting activities by the church.

In addition to planning logistics for identifying and recruiting participants and arranging for meeting space, the four planners for the RiverSouth focus group brainstormed possible topics for the discussion. The team developed the following list of topics, which was later refined and reduced to form the agenda for the session.

1. What kind of music do you like?
2. What is the greatest worry you have?
3. To what magazines do you subscribe?
4. What type of books do read most?
5. What are your favorite TV shows?
6. Which local radio stations do you like?
7. What would you like to see churches doing to help the community?
8. How do you express the spiritual side of your being?
9. If inexpensive seminars were offered near where you live, what subjects would interest you?
10. To what great philosophical questions are you still searching for answers?

Based on this list, the following agenda was built:

Sample Focus Group Agenda **from the River South/Chesterfield County Project**	
6:30 P.M.	Gather, invite attendees to have refreshments
6:40 P.M.	Welcome, State the purpose of the meeting: To secure candid feedback from a representative group of Chesterfield residents on behalf of a new venture locating to the area. "We will be finished by 8:30, and you will receive $50.00 in cash at the close." Introduce focus group facilitator and note-takers.
6:50 P.M.	Ask attendees to complete a one-page, written questionnaire. This information will not be shared with any other organization or enterprise and is confidential
7:00 P.M.	Group discussion starters Advertising • What use do you make of the internet and e-mail during a typical month? • To what adversiting methods do you respond most negatively? (TV, radio, newspaper, flyers, internet, billboards, etc.) • To what adversiting methods do you resond most positively Family Issues • As a parent, what concerns you the most about the future wellbeing of your children? • What do you find most frustrating as a parent? • What activity do you do most with your children? Personal Development • If you suddenly had a four-day work week at the same rate of pay you now get for five days, what would you do with the extra day of time you had available?

	• What, if anything, are you currently doing to develop or enhance your spirituality? • If you were to visit a new church, would you be most interested in a service that was "informal/contemporary" or a service that was "formal/traditional"? World View • What do you think is the greatest threat facing our nation? • Why did you choose to live in the community where you are now living? • What are you doing to contribute to improving the quality of life in the community?
8:15 P.M.	What questions would you like to ask us? We are free to share the name and mission of our client if you would like to know—RiverSouth Community Church. There are cards on the table with the website information about RiverSouth if you are interested.
8:30 P.M.	Final wrap up and payment of participants.

Detailed notes of the focus-group discussion may be taken by a person assisting the facilitator. Some marketers prefer to audio tape or video tape the session. This, of course, should only be done with the knowledge and permission of participants. Others believe that for more informal focus groups, the awareness of a tape recorder or video camera may inhibit the discussion of the group.

Outside Interviews and Shopping Mall Intercepts

Focus groups are useful because valuable information can be gathered by simply asking people questions, but questions can be asked in other settings, too. Area store managers or customer service directors who are sympathetic to a new church venture might be willing to share their own insights and ideas about the marketing profile of area residents. But interviews need not be formal or lengthy. Sometimes these interviews may be done by going door to door, and sometimes they may be more feasibly done by intercepting people in public places, such as shopping malls. In both instances, it is helpful to have a small gift or token—a pocket calendar, coffee mug, ballpoint pen, or gift certificate, perhaps $5.00—to offer people in exchange for giving their time to answer questions. As with outside focus groups, we are asking disinterested people for a segment of their time and attention, and it is reasonable for them to expect something in return.

When Rick Warren began Saddleback Community Church in California, he spent twelve weeks going door to door in the area asking five carefully planned questions:

1. What do you think is the greatest need in this area?
2. Are you actively attending any church?
3. Why do you think most people do not attend church?
4. If you were to look for a church to attend, what kind of things would you look for?
5. What could a congregation in this community do for you? What advice can you give to a congregation that really wants to be helpful to people?[4]

In some communities the door-to-door method of interviewing people is not allowed. In others, it is not well received or welcomed by those who live in the neighborhood. Even in communities where knocking on doors is feasible, great attention should be given to timing. People do not welcome interruptions at dinnertime. They do not appreciate a knock at the door during their favorite TV series or sporting event. I was once part of a community survey effort in which we decided that Saturday mornings would be an ideal time to visit homes. We began our work at 8:30 A.M. After encountering a few angry residents just awakened and in their pajamas, we realized that Saturday morning was not a time to bother hard-working people on their day off. They did not want to be bothered before 11:00 A.M., if at all.

A mall intercept survey (if permission from retailers can be secured) might involve simply stopping people and asking them to answer a few questions The typical conversation might be: "Hello. I am doing a marketing survey for a local organization. I would like to give you this letter opener, hoping that you will give me 90 seconds of your time to answer four brief questions." Be specific about what you are asking people to give, and be careful to keep your end of the bargain.

It is very important to design carefully the four or five questions you will ask. They might be similar to Rick Warren's questions, or they might have a more specific aim in mind. A church wanting to know, for example, whether people in the community would respond to a series of seminars for parents of preschoolers, might ask questions like:

1. Do you have children under the age of six in your home?
2. Would you be interested in receiving helpful information about parenting?
3. If a local organization provided free seminars of this kind on a weeknight, would you attend?
4. What night of the week would be most convenient for you to attend?

One of the advantages of intercept surveys is that the researcher can do some on-the-spot screening of respondents. In the situation just given, for example, the questioner would know not to stop people who were elderly. The questions could be directed to young families and families walking through the mall with young children.

Written Questionnaires

A written questionnaire was utilized with the RiverSouth focus group. It provided some of the needed data about the participants without using up group discussion time. That questionnaire is included as a sample on the following pages.

Sample Focus Group Questionnaire

Name (optional) _____ **Gender** _____

Marital status:
___ never married ___ married with no children ___ divorced
___ married with children

How many years have you lived at your present address?
___ 0–1 ___ 2–4 ___ 5–9 ___ 10+

Number of persons by age in the household:
___ 0–5 ___ 6–10 ___ 11–15 ___ 16–19 ___ 20–25 ___ 26–30
___ 31–35 ___ 36–40 ___41–45 ___ 46–50 ___ 50–65 ___ 65+

Household income:
___ $20–35,000 ___ $35–50,000 ___ $50–75,000
___ $75–100,000 ___ $100–125,000 ___ $125,000+

Education level:
___ high school ___ some college ___ college degre
___ Master's degree ___ Doctoral or professional degree

To what types of music do you listen on a weekly basis?
___ rock ___ easy listening ___ jazz ___ alternative
___ heavy metal ___swing ___ classical ___ country
___ contemporary religious ___ traditional religious

To which *two* local radio stations do you listen most often?
___ XL102 ___ 95.3FM ___ 103.7FM ___92FM ___106.5FM
___ 1140AM ___ Lite 98FM ___ Q94FM other: _____

What cable stations do you watch most?
___ Lifetime ___ ESPN ___ E! ___ MTV ___ TNT ___ USA
___ TBS ___ Discovery ___ Nickelodeon ___ TVLand ___ FAM
___ HGTV ___ TLC ___ CNN ___ MSNBC ___ Fox News
___ CNBC ___ TNN ___ HLN ___ SPDVSN ___ Comedy
other: _____

How many hours a day do you usually watch television?
___ 0–2 ___ 3–4 ___ 5–6 ___ 7+

(continued)

What are your favorite types of books?
___ nonfiction ___ science fiction ___ biographies ___ political
___ mysteries ___ romance ___ thrillers ___ how-to books
___ travel ___ health/medical ___ business/computers
___ investing/finance ___ inspiration/spiritual
other: _____

What types of movies do you prefer?
___ comedy ___ thriller ___ romance ___ drama ___ action
___ foreign ___ children's ___ mystery ___ classics ___ musicals
___ adventure other: _____

What types of cultural events do you attend?
___ symphony ___ opera ___ art galleries ___ ballet
___ musicals ___ plays ___ lectures ___ poetry readings
___ rock concerts ___ country music concerts
___ comedy shows other: _____

Have you attended a church service within the past 30 days?
_____

What are your favorite weekend activities?
___ dining out ___ movies ___ family time ___ shopping
___ television ___ yard work ___ visiting friends ___ parties
___ sporting events other: _____

What are your four favorite outdoor activities?
___ hiking ___ biking ___ running ___ swimming
___ water skiing ___ sailing ___ snow skiing ___ camping
___ gardening ___ caving ___ canoeing/kayaking
___ hunting ___ picnics ___ baseball/softball ___ basketball
___ football ___ soccer ___ volleyball ___ horseback riding
___ rollerblading ___ adventure sports ___ grilling out
other: _____

RiverSouth's Survey Findings

The summary of the written survey of the RiverSouth focus group provided the core church-planting team with some helpful information about their intended niche groups. The typical profile of the focus group was a married person in his or her late thirties or early forties with two teenage children. Their annual income was between $75,000 and $100,000 per year. They held college degrees, and in many instances, graduate degrees. Their favorite radio station was an easy-listening station. The TV channels most watched were cable channels such as CNN, MSNBC, ESPN, and Nickelodeon. Those with smaller children indicated that Nickelodeon was a strong favorite with their kids. The favorite book genres suggested by this focus group were mysteries, thrillers, and other nonfiction. Movie preferences tended toward comedy, action films, and mysteries. Favorite leisure activities were biking, hiking, camping, gardening, and grilling out. It was of interest to note that all of the preferred leisure activities involved the out-of-doors.

The written survey also showed planners that the focus group participants reflected a fairly high level of church involvement. Four of the five in attendance indicated fairly regular and frequent attendance. This indicated another weakness of this focus group effort, in that it was both too small a group and too churched for planners' purposes. The only screening for trying to eliminate churched persons from the group was having it on a Wednesday night. The dilemma here was that if persons were asked about their religious service attendance when enlisted, they may have been tipped off to the possible religious nature of the research, and this might have influenced their response. The notes taken at the focus group discussion were summarized to preserve the information gleaned. The general areas of discussion covered included advertising influences, family or parenting issues, personal or spiritual development, and church style preference.

The group reflected a strong prejudice against telemarketing. At the close of the session, however, when we informed them that we were representing a new church start, a member of the planning team told them that we had just completed two weeks of calling for the church. When she explained the general tone and content of the calls, they indicated that they would not be as negative about calls that were brief and that were quickly identified as church related.

The most consistent form of advertising that seemed to be affirmed by the group was coupons. Four of the five indicated that they clip and use coupons. They look through the newspaper with coupons in mind, and they go through coupon mailings such as Val-Pak. This is interesting since we earlier concluded that Chesterfield residents may be more interested in saving time than money. It should be noted that the people who indicated their interest in coupons are the same people who agreed to come for $50. The general population of the area, and the vast majority of people who did not wish to participate in the focus group, may not be as interested in spending time clipping coupons to save money on purchases. Nevertheless, RiverSouth might want to look at a Val-Pak coupon as a promotional technique.

Parenting was a primary issue for focus group participants. All present in this focus group had children in their homes, and two of the women were stay-at-home moms. A strong and consistent reason given for choosing to live in Chesterfield County was the perceived high quality of the public schools. The group expressed a significant parenting issue as, "I am concerned that other forces and influences in society may be having more impact on the formation of my children's values than I am able to have." High concern was expressed about the breakdown of family life and the dilution of moral values.

The group was evenly divided about whether they would prefer traditional or contemporary church styles. Since they were largely churched persons, their views would not necessarily reflect those of the primary customer base of RiverSouth, unchurched seekers. When asked about their pursuit of spiritual development, several mentioned their attendance in church as a spiritual exercise. Two of the group members spoke about personal prayer and meditation as a part of their spirituality.

This group reflected a fairly high level of involvement in community activities such as scouting, service groups, church-based community ministries, and summer sports activities for children. On the matter of what they would do with any windfall of discretionary time that might come to them, the primary utilization mentioned was running errands and doing essential life chores such as medical appointments, dry-cleaning pickup, grocery shopping, car servicing, and so forth. This reaffirms the conclusion that for these people, time is a precious commodity.

Overall, the focus group provided church planting leaders with basic information and with an awareness that the population in the area was more complex and would be more difficult to reach than originally assumed.

Telephone Surveys

There is considerable debate about the value of telephone surveying in our day. For many people, the early evening interruption of telephone solicitation is an annoyance; however, many organizations continue to utilize telephone contacting. As with other research techniques, the advisability of the method will depend on the circumstances and the skill with which it is utilized. Questions should be brief, responses should be quick and easy, and the intent of the survey should be clear to those doing the research, as well as to those being called.

Telephone calling has been used successfully in preparatory work for the starting of new congregations. Several of the seeker-sensitive new church starts in the country have been launched with telephone survey campaigns. Usually this calling is used to develop a mailing list of persons who express a willingness to receive information about the new congregation. One of the primary values of telephoning is the economy of time and effort required to make many contacts. Many dialups, however, are required for each successful interview that is conducted.

Man-on-the-Street Interviews

I list this method separately from other interview techniques because it is an informal survey method. It does not involve a written questionnaire or a written response. It is done in a way that seems natural and conversational to the respondent. This approach may differ from mall intercepts in that it is more informal and conversational. The researcher does not have a prepared set of questions to address, but rather a general idea of topics about which to converse.

One way to get an understanding of how the congregation may be perceived in the community is to simply ask people in the area if they know of the congregation, where it is located, or what their impression of that faith community is. I have enjoyed, through the years, arriving at a community where I was to lead a conference or consultation, and simply asking a person on the sidewalk or in a store about the location of the church. It is amazing how often people who live within a mile of a congregation's meeting place will have no idea that it exists. I have asked people, "What do you think about that church?" and gotten answers like: "Oh, they are always fighting with each other," "They really pitch in when someone in the community has a need," or "I think the mayor is a member there."

Research conducted in this way, of course, is not scientifically verifiable, but it can provide helpful soft data and give church leaders new insights into how they are perceived. To be more reliable, the question asked should be worded to solicit an answer that is as objective as possible, and the same question should be asked in the same way of each respondent.

Observational Research

Observational research is an indirect approach. No face-to-face contact is required, and no communication is exchanged. It is research based on people watching or windshield surveys of a community, or billboard analysis. People watching might involve simply sitting in a public place where people are going about their business and observing the appearance, dress, mood, and other characteristics of people. A windshield survey means driving up and down the streets of an area to be surveyed to observe as many characteristics as possible about the community. Some of the things to watch for might be:

1. How well is housing maintained?
2. Do homes appear to be owner occupied or rentals?
3. What evidence is observable of crime and security problems?
4. Are there swing sets or sand boxes in yards (indicating presence of small children)?
5. Are there bicycles in yards or on porches (indicating older children)?
6. What evidence do you see of new development in the area? Is it residential or commercial?
7. Is there a great deal of multifamily housing in the area?
8. What age brackets (these might be noted in terms of decade guesses about the ages of people; for example, 0–10 years, 10–20 years, and so forth) of residents do you observe as you drive around the area?
9. What do you observe that indicates racial diversity in the area?
10. Does the community seem to be receiving adequate public services (for example, streets, police, or fire)?
11. What do you observe that indicates litter and trash problems?

12. Does the community show evidence of alcohol or drug abuse? Does there seem to be an unusually large number of bars and liquor stores, or do people on the street appear to be loitering or under the influence of drugs or alcohol?
13. Do you observe sufficient public places for children and youth to play?
14. Does there appear to be adequate public transportation, or are pedestrian facilities safe and convenient for use by persons who may not have an automobile?

In many areas, evaluating advertising and billboards reveals information about the community. Often the secular advertisers who focus on a certain area and invest in billboard advertising know who lives there and what will appeal to them. The church may be able to learn a great deal by observing the competition for the attention and involvement of people.

Church researchers may wish to use the following survey form for billboard research. Church members or leaders may be enlisted to drive the main highways or boulevards that are commonly driven by the people who live in the communities they want to better understand. There should always be at least two people in the car; otherwise, this exercise could be very dangerous. The driver should concentrate on driving while passengers study the billboards and complete the form.

Notes on Billboard Observations in Target Areas

(What do secular advertisers know that we need to know?)

Complete a separate copy of this form for each billboard viewed. Drive carefully!

What product or service is being advertised?

_____

What does the advertiser hope to accomplish?

_____

What is the basis for appeal (for example, success, security, or sex)?

_____

What is the primary image? Is it text only?

_____

What are the dominant colors used?

_____

What font style is used for text?

_____

What is your initial emotional response?

_____

High-Tech Research Applications

The Internet is an important research tool; there are ways to identify potential groups for ministry focus and outreach by using Web sites, chat rooms, and other possibilities. Browsing Web sites on subjects of interest to certain niche groups, and visiting chat rooms where certain topics are discussed, may lead to ideas for outreach. Though the current discussion focuses primarily on outside research, it might also be noted here that some of the inside research conducted by congregations could easily be conducted by e-mail if a large portion of the membership utilize e-mail. Questionnaires can be posted to Web sites and downloaded for completion by respondents. There are many creative possibilities for computer-based research to gather outside data as well as inside data.

The readiness for these newer methods will vary from church to church, but if there is a task force or team in the church working on the research process, the brainstorming of that group may result in many innovative approaches. When we ask ourselves what we need to learn from secular experts, certainly the potential of the Internet is a growing enterprise for those in marketing and sales.

An Overview of the Market-Driven Ministry Process

The bottom line for any market analysis process is to learn how congregations can better read their cultural context and design ways of impacting their communities for Christ. The entire process might be understood as:

- *Read* the context of the church. Study the community and learn who is there and what they need.
- *Relate* to those you hope to reach. Sometimes it means changing your traditional ways of doing things if you are to more effectively build relationships with those persons.
- *Reach* beyond your traditional ways of doing things in order to connect with new people. Find the ways you can reach out to those who need what you can offer.

- *Reshape* the structures and methods of your church as necessary. Empower and equip the laity to develop innovative approaches to touching the lives of new people.
- *Release* the people to do new things. Churches can be permission-giving or permission-withholding. The future belongs to permission-giving churches.

Once a congregation has gathered information from within its membership, and has supplemented that information with the reading of their context by gathering community data, congregational leaders may move toward identifying niche possibilities and developing strategies.

5

The Who and How of Niche Marketing

Once information has been gathered about the congregation's identity and strengths, as well as information about the needs present in the context, there are decisions to be made. The task force will use that information to decide, among all the possibilities, specifically who the congregation will attempt to reach and how.

Who Needs What Your Congregation Can Provide?

There are people who are waiting to receive what your congregation has to offer. The tasks of market-driven planning are to determine who these people are, where they are, what they need, and how to best meet their needs. This draws us to the marketing disciplines of marketing segmentation and target marketing.

Sarah White, the author of *The Complete Idiot's Guide to Marketing Basics*, writes, "Market segmentation is the way marketers respond to the fact that different groups of customers have different wants and needs. A large heterogeneous market is divided into segments that share certain characteristics."[1] Large, diverse populations can be analyzed and addressed more specifically by dividing them into homogeneous segments. The segments can be based on any of the myriad of categories covered by the census data. These may include: age brackets, gender, income level, education level, marital status, race or ethnicity, housing type, and household type as shown in samples in the previous chapter.

Marketing research companies supplement the census data categories with many additional categories of information. These may include lifestyle characteristics, travel habits, product preferences, investment tendencies, religious preferences, and an infinite number of other segment definitions. Theoretically, if an organization wanted to determine the number, within their community, of left-handed, young adult, Presbyterian males, living alone, who watch ESPN, and drive Toyotas pickups, that information is probably available. If it is not already available based on completed research, there are organizations that will be happy to do the research to determine that or any other conceivable segment.

Once segments are identified, the task becomes one of getting more information about each niche group of people and coming to better understand each of these population segments. According to White, "Target marketing means identifying a specific segment of the general public who are more likely to buy your offering, then directing your marketing activity toward influencing that targeted group."[2] Once congregation leaders have a deeper understanding of the people who compose the niche, ministries can be designed to meet their needs. The marketing question to be answered then is, "How can we best package what we have to offer to appeal to the people who form this segment?"

These extraordinary efforts to understand and appeal to a segment are easily justifiable for a company selling a product. Appealing to a segment of the market, even a narrow segment, may involve the sale of thousands of units of a product that would otherwise not be sold. It could make the difference between financial success or failure for a company. But should congregations be doing this? White says, "Nonprofit organizations serve two audiences: donors and recipients are among the terms used. Target marketing is extremely relevant for non-profits."[3] Therefore, congregations will want to identify segments that have needs they can address, and they will design ministries and services to meet those needs. The difference between profit and loss for commercial enterprises relates to their effectiveness in selling a product. For congregations the issue is not profit or loss; it is the effectiveness with which they relate to segments of the population in their area that determines their growth or decline.

In many ways, congregations are more complex and provide a more demanding leadership challenge than the average business. Congregations have several categories of customers. As White noted about nonprofits, there are the donors or supporting members of the organization who must be served, but there are also the recipients for ministry that must be considered primary customers. When researchers ask congregational leaders, "Who is your customer?" the answers given include: all our members, our resident members, our Sunday visitors, everyone in the community, the people who give the money, the unchurched of the region, those who have needs, and all the people of the world. It is a task of the congregation to clarify and find consensus about who those persons are who most need what they have to offer.

Marketing Process Design

Once a church identifies the segments of the population it is attempting to reach, there are some questions to be addressed. *The Portable MBA in Marketing*, written by Alexander Hiam and Charles D. Schewe, suggests five important questions to consider:

1. Can the market segment be identified and measured?
2. Is the segment large enough to be worthwhile?
3. Is the segment reachable?
4. Is the segment responsive?
5. Is the segment stable?[4]

These questions are a reminder that some otherwise interesting segments may not have good potential for congregational focus. A segment may be too small to really offer the church a great opportunity for meaningful service; for example, a church might find that there are a few dozen people in their area who do not have medical insurance or healthcare. They might determine that healthcare coverage is a real need, but discover that they do not have the resources available to meet the need. The church may wish to look for referral options and community services to help such people, but determine that it is not a segment for which they can provide direct services.

Some segments may be so unresponsive that they simply cannot be penetrated; or, a segment may be very transitional. A congregation might lay great plans for ministering to a youth subculture, only to see fads change and that segment disappear.

Author Jennifer Lawton, in writing "The Two Faces of Niche Marketing," suggests an alternative process for approaching niche marketing. She counseled the organization designing niche strategies:

1.   Know yourself. Know your strengths and how best to use them.
2.   Know your goal. Have a clear sense of what you hope to achieve.
3.   Know your customer. Understand your niche and its felt needs.
4.   Keep it simple. Make your strategy as straightforward and understandable as possible.
5.   Have Fun! Utilize humor and adventure in your pursuit of new niches.[5]

Lawton's five points provide a simple way for congregations to measure their readiness to engage in niche strategies. Her emphasis on fun allows for creativity, experimentation, and an openness to trying things that might fail.

There are two other principles to keep in mind as a congregation moves into niche marketing. One is that the organization must achieve absolute excellence in what it offers its niche. In an article titled "Prospering in a Niche Market," author Pat Means writes, "Once established, a niche business must dominate its market. In a niche, Number One is the only place to be. You don't have the luxury of languishing in fifth place."[6] A second principle of importance is that there must be a passion for the niche on the part of someone involved in the new ministry. This personal passion gives the individual or team leading the effort motivation as well as direction. [7]

In the context of congregations, I interpret *excellence* to mean that things are done with strong attention to quality. The design of the ministries, the care with which they are carried out, and the ways in which they are promoted and publicized—all will reflect that concern for quality. That kind of quality is reflected in the appearance of the facilities, materials, and persons who conduct ministry, the professionalism with which they do their work, and the careful attention to detail in their pursuit of their mission. The issue of passion for congregations deals with the spirit that is an essential element of the community of faith. This is the inner fire that drives the follower of God.

An Intrapreneurial Enterprise

It will often be an intrapreneur who will seek to redirect and revitalize the life of an organization by applying niche marketing. While entrepreneurs generally start new things, intrapreneurs are people who work within existing organizations to revitalize and redirect them. In the context of church life, entrepreneurs are church planters, and intrapreneurs are pastors and lay leaders who guide established churches with longstanding traditions and customs. Intrapreneurs, however, work within established organizations with their own sense of vision and purpose. These persons strive to accomplish effective change without destroying the organization or violating its heritage. Gifford Pinchot described the intrapreneurial leader as someone who:

1. is a team builder
2. has a firm grasp of business and marketplace reality
3. can make fast decisions without much data or guidance
4. is action oriented
5. does not like to take no for an answer
6. will do mundane work to move a project along quickly[8]

These descriptions of the intrapreneur create some uneasiness with many. When we hear about the need to make fast decisions without much data, it sounds risky. When we consider an intrapreneur being action oriented and not taking no for an answer, it sounds like a violation of the very principle of team building espoused in Pinchot's first point. The key to embracing all of these seeming contradictions is to find the right balance of teamwork and individual initiative, of rapid response and sound decision making, and of action and reflection.

The aspiring intrapreneur will need to learn and utilize several skills. First, the intrapreneur must be a person willing to experiment; that is, to take risks in the development of new approaches.[9] Although the strategy for a new effort, such as niche marketing in the church, must be carefully planned, leaders should be able to quickly abandon failing projects and learn the lessons available from failed experiments.

An intrapreneur must be a masterful change agent. "The individuals who will succeed and flourish will . . . be managers of change: adept at reorienting their own and others' activities in untried directions to bring about higher levels of achievement."[10] A congregational leader or a team of leaders moving a congregation toward market-driven planning and niche ministry must be able to convince church decision makers to value innovation and embrace constructive change. The leaders will persuade the constituency to embrace the plan, then lead them skillfully through a carefully crafted process of making the changes required. For congregations, the higher levels of achievement will be reflected in greater effectiveness in empowering and enabling the laity to serve the needs of the recipients of niche ministries.

Finally, an intrapreneur must be able to find low-cost ways to accomplish excellent marketing. Few traditional congregations are prepared to pay large amounts of money for market research and advertising. The answer is to find creative ways of doing good work in those areas without spending huge amounts of money. In a book entitled, *Guerilla Marketing: Secrets for Making Big Profits from Your Small Business*, marketing expert Jay Levinson referred to this creative, economical approach as guerilla marketing. He said that the following principles apply to guerilla marketing:

1. If your congregation is small, consider your size an ally. Small organizations can (theoretically) move more quickly and be more flexible.
2. You must have quality. No matter how good the promotion or how creatively financed the campaign, it is useless unless what is offered is of superior quality.
3. You must constantly monitor what works and what does not work. Do not waste resources on what does not work.
4. Go all out. Exploit every opportunity for marketing. Many of the most helpful marketing methods will not involve paid advertising. Congregations may be able to secure feature stories about their projects rather than paid ads. Radio and TV stations may have community service announcements that save purchasing time on air.
5. Have all marketing pulling in the same direction. Build it all around a "core concept."[11] A congregation might promote all of its niche efforts under a motto such as, "A Church That Cares About People." This theme could run through every individual niche effort being made by the congregation and serve as the banner under which all efforts could be promoted. RiverSouth Church adopted the motto, "Connecting People with God and with One Another." That theme of creating relational connections was applied to every outreach and ministry.

Examples of Possible Niche Markets

Marketers have attempted to categorize the potential segments under three large groups. Utilizing a system called VALS (Values and LifeStyles), they identified the need-driven segment, the outer-directed segment, and the inner-directed segment. These three groups are then broken down into nine subcategories.

Need-Driven
- Survivor: the very poor, struggling to pay the bills, having a focus on the daily necessities.
- Sustainer: poor, angry, resentful, often minorities, lacking education, but not necessarily as deep in poverty as the survivors.

Outer-Directed
- Belonger: Aging, traditional, patriotic, high-school graduates, solid citizens.
- Emulator: Ambitious, competitive, emulating the more affluent, status symbol conscious.
- Achiever: Successful, materialistic, middle aged, many college educated. (Not generally as obsessed with status symbols as the emulators.)

Inner-Directed
- I-Am-Me: Young, impulsive, active, college educated but lower income.
- Experiential: Youthful, artistic, seeking direct experience, personal development, affluent.
- Socially Conscious: Mature, successful, socially active, highly educated, mission oriented.
- Integrated: Psychologically mature, open-minded and understanding.[12]

These and other systems of categorizing market segments may be helpful for congregational application. Sometimes we have attempted to meet needs that people did not have, or at least did not feel they had. The outreach methodology of the congregation will be different for Survivors than it will be for the Socially Conscious. A congregation will provide practical assistance of immediate benefit to serve the Survivors; they will offer more meaning-giving and personal fulfillment opportunities for the Socially Conscious.

The niche marketing possibilities for a congregation will be constantly changing due to the rapid pace of change in society. Sarah White suggests: a vision of the future with new market niches that offer exciting potential. You don't need supernatural powers to guess that America is changing, and a big part of that change (putting it bluntly) is that Baby Boomers are getting old. The market for products and services of value to older life stages is going to grow like topsy.[13] This vision can be viewed as good news for congregations that are prepared to be sensitive to the development of new niches and the needs and interests that those niches will have.

There is considerable interest, due to the rapid pace of change these days, in anticipating what may be coming in the future. Congregations may face new and different challenges as they move on in the 21st century. When asked to speculate about what some of the new niches for the new millennium may be, White offered the following list of possible emerging niche markets:

1.   Persons pursuing lifelong learning. There will be increasing interest in adult education and personal growth.
2.   Persons interested in maintaining good health. Boomers want to live long and well.
3.   Persons interested in financial products and services. Investing and achieving security are important to boomers.
4.   People who are considering retirement housing and remodeling for adaptation to the needs of the aging.
5.   People who are interested in travel and leisure activity.[14]

As I look over that list, it impresses me that religious congregations are in a good position to address all of those possible emerging niches. Faith communities have been about education for centuries, and are uniquely equipped to offer relevant lifelong learning opportunities. Within the membership of many (even small and midsize) congregations, there are dedicated believers who are prepared to lead conferences and provide services in matters of health, financial planning, and aging adjustments. The groups that White's list seems to omit are the "lost fragments" mentioned earlier in chapter 4. It should be noted that poverty will not go away, and congregations will not be fulfilling their mission if they only seek to minister to the middle class and above.

The increasing emphasis on travel and leisure offerings means that congregations may move toward budgeting, programming, and staffing to meet this interest. Even some small churches are beginning to employ a coordinator to arrange and sponsor leisure events for older adults. This provision of a person, paid or volunteer, to plan and conduct worthwhile travel and activities lets a church address the needs of a potential niche group. In much the same way that churches have long worked to provide meaningful activities and ministry opportunities for youth, the demand is growing for similar opportunities for senior adults. The persons who make up these niches have great potential to become ministry providers, as well as recipients. While the congregation may look upon them as persons to be served, they also have great potential to become servants of God and of God's work. An example of this might be an overseas travel opportunity for senior adults that has an element of mission work attached to traveling. While a group is seeing Mexico City, they might take two days to clean and paint the dormitory of an orphanage. This allows the recipients of niche ministry to become providers of ministry to others.

Having addressed the matter of who may be doing niche marketing and who the focus of some of those efforts may be, we are left with the big question of, "How?" How shall congregations successfully mobilize themselves to reach niches?

The How of Niche Marketing: Finding the Open Gates

I grew up on a farm, and as a teenager I was responsible for a small herd of dairy cows. We frequently would need to move the herd from one pasture to another for grazing. Each pasture had a gate large enough to accommodate the passage of a tractor. To get the cows into the new area, we would open the gate, then drive the herd right toward the gate. It was amazing how many times they could not find the access to the fresh grazing. They were so accustomed to the gate being closed that they had paradigm blindness, which prevented them from seeing that it was now open. Usually after herding them toward the open gate several times, they would finally see it and go in.

There are open gates that will provide you better access to the niche group with which you hope to connect. Your efforts to communicate with a given market segment will be frustrating until you find the open gate. Understanding the mindset of the niche group and knowing something about their values and lifestyle can help you to identify the most effective and efficient ways to gain access to their attention.

The project conducted at University Heights Baptist Church resulted in the identification of some niches and some possible new strategies for touching those groups. Following are some of their niches and strategies as samples:

Niche 1: Musicians and others who appreciate the fine arts. These are prospects for outreach and increased involvement in the congregation.

1. Special events at the church might be promoted through the publications at the universities. These might be paid ads or they might be available occasionally as public service announcements.
2. Musical and other fine-arts activities at the church should be promoted through the fine-arts departments at the schools, and on some occasions the university departments will be involved in the presentations.
3. The church might consider forming its major annual musical and drama presentations into a concert series. The concert series could be promoted with a specially prepared brochure and posters that would include multiple events.
4. The church should promote its concert series or other major activities with large banners displayed on the church property. These banners can be purchased for reasonable costs, and they can be displayed temporarily without the typical hassles with local government regulations. National Avenue and Grand Street are busy enough thoroughfares to give the church considerable visibility for such banners.

Niche 2: Incoming corporate management personnel new to Springfield. These persons would be prospects for outreach and enlistment.

1. Network with the Chamber of Commerce and read the Springfield Business Journal to get the names of new business leaders moving to Springfield. Contact them by mail to welcome them to the area and make them aware of UHBC.
2. Network with local realtors to secure the names of persons moving into the affluent neighborhoods south and southeast of the church.
3. Be aware that Baptists and others coming from northern states, the northeast, Virginia, North Carolina and Texas may tend to be moderate and more interested in UHBC.

Niche 3: Young couples and families with small children. These families would be prospects for outreach and enlistment.

1. Maintain the highest quality of childcare and programming for young children. Provide childcare for all services and programs where young families are expected to attend.

2. Consider the offering of a Mother's Day Out service for young families.
3. Regularly offer parenting courses, marriage enrichment workshops, and other programs of interest to young couples.
4. Consider enhancing the church's ministry to couples desiring to use the church for weddings. This may require the enlistment of a wedding coordinator (paid for by a fee built into the church's wedding charges) and other ministers to assist the pastor with weddings. In addition to the premarital classes already offered, each couple should have one session with one of the ministers to explore the matter of a shared faith and a shared church home as a marriage-strengthening element. The church may also wish to offer a rotating series of Sunday Bible studies for persons preparing for marriage, and the provision of a mentor couple to share their marriage experience with each couple. These studies could help create a bridge for interested couples to get started in Sunday school and to get acquainted at UHBC.

Niche 4: International students staying in Springfield. This group would be recipients of ministry more than prospects for membership.

1. Continue to work with the Baptist Student Union and other groups to offer needed services and ministries to international students. Network with the universities and colleges to provide services that may be otherwise overlooked.
2. Focus on the opportunity for visitation in a typical American home as a service to international students. This particular opportunity may be best provided through a church, which also creates the occasion to share the faith orientation of an American family with those from other cultures.
3. Have an annual occasion at the church that honors and highlights international students and visitors from other countries.
4. Work with local corporate and government structures to help provide needed services for foreign visitors who may be coming for a period of time.

Niche 5: Single mothers with school-age children. There are nearly 5,000 single-mother families living within a five-mile radius of the church. This would be a group for ministry services rather than being likely prospects for membership. This niche, as any niche group, should only be addressed by UHBC if there are church members who feel a calling and a passion for helping these families.

1. Offer assistance with childcare, tutoring of children, mentoring of mothers, big-brother male friends for boys, big-sister female friends for girls, and other services for single moms.
2. Provide parenting training and support groups for single mothers.
3. Let the community know that UHBC cares about single mothers through press releases, community-service announcements, and feature stories for the media.
4. Work with local social services to identify unmet needs and underserved persons who fit this niche.

These examples show how a congregation may articulate its intentions of touching certain niche groups, and how they can brainstorm and strategize to find ways to attempt to reach them.

Ministry or Evangelistic Outreach

Once data is gathered both from inside the congregation and from the broader community, informed decisions can be made about the niche groups that the church will attempt to touch. It should be noted, however, that church outreach has two distinct purposes. One primary purpose is to minister to persons who have needs. This is done from compassion and as an expression of the love and grace of the living God. We follow God's example when we give ourselves to meeting the needs of people around us.

When congregations design strategies for reaching out in ministry, they need to keep in mind that this kind of outreach is done simply to help people. It should not be evaluated in terms of what the congregation stands to get out of it. We help the hurting because it is the right thing to do; it is the God-like thing to do. We expect nothing in return for ourselves or for the faith community. When we engage in ministry, we do not expect to receive members for the congregation or dollars for the offering plate in return. For example, when a congregation provides a ministry to homeless people, the services rendered are a gift given without any expectation of a benefit coming back to the congregation.

A second type of congregational outreach is evangelism. When we engage in evangelistic outreach we may, in fact, be looking toward inviting persons as followers of the faith, and as members of the congregation. (I use the word *evangelism* in this context to mean the efforts of the community of faith to share their religious concepts with the hope that persons may embrace those beliefs, enter into a spiritual relationship with God, and become a part of the faith community.) When we do ministry, we hope it will result in evangelism, and when we do evangelism, we hope it will involve ministry to people. While these two may go together very well and may often overlap, it is important to distinguish between them as primary motivations when we look at niche marketing.

Niche marketing for congregations is an effort to become more specific and specialized in outreach to persons in the communities around the congregation. This requires that we be clear about what our goals are in addressing a given niche. We hope to share a positive witness with those to whom we minister, but it may be unrealistic to expect that ministry will result in persons joining our congregation. They may decide, as they follow God's leading, to join another congregation. Ministry outreach must be done with a broader view of God's purposes. We do it for the sake of God's mission, not expecting a benefit to our own religious organization. Such ministry shows a high view of God's purposes, and it also indicates a respect for the uniqueness and dignity of each individual.

Congregations also need to grow. The desire of God and the mandate of the Scriptures are for the people of God to experience health and growth in their pursuit of God's purposes. A congregation needs to reach new people who will pursue its faith, find fellowship in that congregation, grow in its spiritual practice, become contributing members of the congregation, and assume roles of service and leadership. This natural process of growth is not primarily for the institutional survival of the congregation, but for the enrichment of the lives of people. However, it is a reality that for the good work to continue through a given congregation, it must survive. When pursuing evangelistic outreach of this kind, it is appropriate for congregation leaders to evaluate their efforts by asking, "Is this project yielding the results and benefits to the congregation that we envisioned when we launched it?"

When we design strategies for congregational expansion and later evaluate them, we can and should ask ourselves whether the desired growth is taking place. "Are we seeing increased confirmations or baptisms, new members and increased offerings as a result of this effort? Are we seeing an increase in the quality of the spiritual lives of our members?" When we design strategies that are primarily aimed at meeting needs and helping the hurting, we use a different set of criteria. It will be perfectly all right for those ministries if they never bring one new member to the congregation or translate into one new dollar in the offering plate. If we are clear about these distinctions in purpose as we design the strategies, we can sharpen and enhance our ways of accomplishing both ministry and evangelism.

University Heights Baptist Church is a city congregation located adjacent to a university campus. The church has a high level of educational attainment among its members, a strong music program, and a fairly traditional approach to worship and church programming. Worship includes excellent organ music, an accomplished choir, a good handbell choir, and frequent performance of classical religious music by instrumentalists. Sunday services feature a choral anthem, congregational hymn singing, and a sermon by the pastor.

When we took a careful look at the demographics for a five-mile radius around the church, one of the interesting things we discovered was a particular zip code area that had a number of single mothers with children at home that was almost double the national average. There were nearly 5,000 households of this composition in the church area, and most of them were within this one zip code area near the church. The question for the church was, "Is this a niche group that our church wants to try to serve?"

If the answer to that question is yes, then we ask ourselves the second equally important question, "Would this best be started as a caring ministry or as a church-growth outreach?" Assume that the church decides that the best approach to the beginning of such work would be as a ministry to need, not as a church-growth effort. That means the ministry should not be evaluated based on how many new members it produces. That emphasis, and indeed the results, might change later in the development of the effort, but initially it would be understood as a ministry designed to serve an otherwise underserved element of the community.

What Strategies Will Help Us Reach These People?

As you observed in the examples from University Heights Baptist Church, each group identified specified whether the niche was primarily a target for ministry by the church or if it had strong potential for church outreach and membership growth. Then there were suggestions of possible marketing methods for serving and communicating with each niche.

It should be clearly understood that when we speak of niches, we are not intending to be exclusive of anyone. All persons seeking God were welcome at UHBC regardless of race, gender, socioeconomic level, or life circumstance. This report was internal to the church leadership, and it was not intended to create or maintain an elitist congregation.

As a church begins to focus on a niche, it is time to apply the principles of market-based strategy. In *Segmentation Marketing*, John Berrigan and Carl Finkbeiner offered the following list of tasks: develop your general message, develop segment-specific positioning messages, design key-people positioning messages, select the best media for getting the message out, and provide multiple entry points.

1.   Develop a general message. The congregation needs to prepare a statement that indicates why it is the congregation that is uniquely concerned and able to meet the needs of the niche group. The statement may say, "We are a church that cares about families."

2.   Develop segment-specific positioning messages. That is, while a church may describe itself in one way to one segment it is seeking to reach, it may have a totally different way of presenting itself to other segments. The message should be segment specific. The general message will express the big-picture description of the church, but it will be supplemented by more specific messages that apply to individual segments. For example, the general message mentioned above might be made more specific to apply to the narrower niche group. That statement might be, "We offer unique services for single parents and their children."

3.   Design key-people positioning messages. Develop a profile of the typical person who would be representative of the segment. Get to know that profile, and develop an awareness of who this person is, and what this person's problems and gifts may be. Create a specific personal message from the congregation to that individual. That message might be, "If you are feeling overwhelmed by the challenge of raising children alone, we care about you and have services and resources to help you."

4.   Select the best media for getting the message out. Once a niche is identified, it should be easier to develop a media strategy that will be more effective for reaching that group. Some niche groups can best be addressed through newspaper ads, others through radio or television, and others through direct mail. The use of the telephone, door-to-door contact, and other methods should be considered. For every niche, there are preferred ways to make contact. The study of the niche characteristics and demographic details will provide information about which forms of media are most utilized by members of the niche. Advertising can be directed through the media outlets (for example, radio, television, cable, or newspaper) that will most efficiently reach the niche.

5.   Provide multiple entry points. It is always best if there is more than one way offered for a niche person to connect with the church. In the case of single mothers, a number of services might be made available. These could include a mothers' shopping day, free childcare time on Saturday, a series of seminars on parenting alone, a big-brother mentoring program, after-school tutoring, and a workshop on child safety in the neighborhood.[15]

Planning the Advertising

Once a strategy is in place for the ministries that will be offered to a niche group, the advertising or promotion of their availability must be designed. Advertising is one small element in the total marketing effort, and it is the one that, by definition, always has a financial cost attached. Marketers usually begin their advertising efforts by studying what the competition is doing to advertise.[16] In the church context, this might include seeking answers to such questions as the following:

1.   What other churches are serving this niche, and how are they advertising?
2.   If no other churches are specializing in this area, are there any community agencies doing so? How are they reaching the niche?
3.   What can be learned from the school system, the social welfare system, or other community groups about how to best communicate with this niche?
4.   What are businesses doing to reach this market segment?
5.   Is this niche group fairly definable in terms of geographic location?

6. Is this niche known to frequent particular stores or locales in the community?
7. Do people in this niche tend to prefer print or broadcast media?

A congregation's budget for advertising may be limited. The task then becomes how to accomplish maximum effective promotion with minimum investment in advertising. Advertising for a congregational event or ministry will incorporate the five principles listed earlier under the section, "What strategies will help us reach these people?" It will be designed to appeal to the specific need of a definable niche. Whether its goal is to do ministry or outreach, advertising niche-ministry activities is useful to a congregation.

Congregations can save money by using some of the following "guerilla" tactics:

1. Make use of the free announcement services available for congregational events. Most radio and TV stations and most newspapers have community calendar services that disseminate this type of information.
2. Ask for discounts for advertising purchased by the congregation. Most media outlets have standard discounts that are provided for nonprofit and community service organizations; however, you may not get the discount if you do not request it.
3. Get competitive bids and do comparison shopping when placing advertising.
4. Develop a personal relationship with the religion editors of local papers. These persons decide which persons, projects, and congregations will be featured in newspaper stories. If you develop a pattern of providing the editor with good ideas and leads for interesting stories, your credibility will help you get stories in the paper related to the work of your congregation.
5. Have a public-relations team in the church continually keep current announcements on community bulletin boards.
6. Utilize regional and shopping papers in your area. These publications often reach your target group more efficiently, and their advertising rates are much lower. They are often hungry for good public-interest stories.
7. If the congregation's building is located in a highly visible place or on a major traffic route, the use of banners can accomplish a great deal of

inexpensive advertising for events. Some congregations find that they can have the benefit of a billboard for the small cost of having a large banner printed to hang on their church or on the lawn. Sometimes local zoning rules interfere with these possibilities, but usually a congregation is allowed to temporarily hang a banner on its own building.

8.   Investigate the possibility of being a day sponsor on your local public radio station. These stations do not usually sell advertising, but they often will accept day sponsorships that include a certain number of mentions of the sponsoring individual or group during the day. The fee for this sponsorship is usually quite reasonable.

The Expression and Impression Paradox

When congregations begin to plan promotional communication, it is always important to recognize that what one thinks he or she is saying is not always what others are hearing. Marketing is a combination of expressions and impressions. Communicators plan what they intend to express, but they must also find ways to assess the impression that message will have on the recipient.

Congregations should develop ways to monitor their communications to catch unintended and unexpected impressions they may be having on people. The book *Marketing Aesthetics* tells about the longstanding problem with public perception that Proctor & Gamble has had. They spent years fighting rumors about satanism being represented in their logo, and persistent rumors that their CEO was donating large amounts of company profit to his satanic church. All of this was untrue. The rumors were finally traced to a competitor, and in 1995 a lawsuit was filed by Proctor & Gamble. It could be noted, however, that the problem was not entirely due to malicious intent and deliberate deception. The company did have a logo that lent credibility to the rumors: an antiquated logo with various symbols that were subject to misinterpretation contributed to the problem. They were giving an impression they did not want or intend to give.[17]

Because perception and image are important parts of how congregations are understood in this culture, the advertising and promotion they do for their niche marketing efforts should be carefully scrutinized. A congregation that says, "We are *the* congregation in town that cares for children" is communicating an arrogance and a disregard for other local faith groups in the community that may be inaccurate and self-defeating. A congregation can highlight its excellence and strength without claiming comparative superiority to all other congregations. One church has an annual week of volunteerism during which it enlists a majority of their members in a myriad of community service projects. The projects in which they engage are publicized in the press, and frequently there are human-interest stories about people who have been helped. This is an example of how the expression (the objective message of what is being done) is positive, and the impression (the visceral response of those who hear about it) is also positive.

One of the potential benefits of niche marketing for faith communities might be a lessening of some of the unhealthy competition that has existed among churches and denominations. If, within the work of God's church on earth, it were decided that some congregations could best minister to certain types of people and that others could best evangelize other types of people, the total faith community would function with the complementary and supportive elements that God desires for people. That larger view of God's mission can help congregations function with a greater sense of partnership with others and with greater confidence that they can make a difference.

Congregations willing to put the time and energy into understanding their own strengths and resources, willing to study their communities to locate people with specific needs, and willing to create new strategies for reaching those people, shall find those efforts well rewarded. The task of market-driven planning can be organized into a process that church leaders will be able to adjust contextually and apply in their setting. Chapter 6 offers such a process.

6

A Sample Process for Developing a Niche Marketing Plan

There is no fixed formula for applying niche marketing principles to a congregation's outreach or ministry program. What is suggested in this chapter is a sample, not a recipe. It is intended to be a generic process that can be adapted to use in a specific situation. That adaptation may involve changing the process in many ways. For example, in a smaller congregation, the generic process may be shortened and simplified due to the smaller number of people involved. A larger congregation may have some organizational systems already in place that may need to be included in the design process.

The sample process is divided into seven phases: preparation, research, niche selection, strategy design, marketing design, implementation, and evaluation. Each phase includes two to four action steps to complete, with a total of 21 steps to the entire process. The time frame spanned by such a process might be anywhere from two to six months or longer.

To provide an overview of the entire process, the chart on the following pages will provide that "snapshot." Then, the process will be expanded and described in detail.

Niche Marketing Planning Process

Preparation Phase
1. Secure support of the primary leaders.
2. Determine budget for research and initial marketing.
3. Create or designate a task force to guide the process.

Research and Discovery Phase
4. Determine inside research approaches and delegate tasks.
5. Determine outside research approaches and delegate tasks.
6. Hear reports from all research groups.
7. Analyze church strengths and potential niche groups.

Niche Selection Phase
8. Determine feasibility and priority of various niches.
9. Determine the level of passion for various niches.
10. Select niches for immediate attention and those for later work.

Strategy Design Phase
11. Design methods and means for niche group to be addressed.
12. Develop minimum necessary structure to conduct the ministry.

Marketing Design Phase
13. Apply research to design a marketing plan for launching.
14. Allocate resources for the project and its promotion.
15. Set launch date for project and enlist congregational affirmation.

Implementation Phase
16. Begin the work.
17. Adjust the game plan and continue the work.

Evaluation and Adaptation Phase
18. Secure evaluation of the ministry from those conducting it.
19. Secure evaluation from those who have been recipients.
20. Compile the lessons learned.

Preparation Phase

1.   Secure the support of the primary leadership structure or of the congregation as a whole. The consultant or initiator of the niche-marketing idea will need to have an informational meeting with the congregational leaders. If an outside consultant is not used, the congregational leader (clergy) might serve as the facilitator; or a layperson with experience in marketing, strategic planning, or organizational management might serve in this role. Once the appropriate board or committee believes that a niche-marketing plan for the congregation should be developed, action can be taken by the congregation's administrative structure to give the project official blessing. For some congregations, this may also include securing approval from a judicatory or denominational office. Every setting is different, and the most desirable way to receive official sanction for the effort will vary.

This step is important in order to avoid having the sense emerge later that the clergy, staff, or some board of the congregation is making unauthorized and inappropriate decisions about the congregation's future. The entire process becomes more palatable for all members and partners of the faith community if it has prior approval for exploration. Leaders should also keep in mind the importance having buy-in by the informal leadership of the congregation. These are people who may be unofficial and unelected, but leaders nonetheless. A preparatory process of education may be involved, but the time invested up front in securing the blessing of stakeholders is well worth the cost.

2.   Determine a budget for the research aspect of the effort and for the first round of marketing. There may be funds already budgeted for advertising, church promotion, demographic research, and so forth. For many congregations, however, this may be an entirely new area of financial need. It will be helpful later if an official blessing of the congregation, mentioned in step 1, has been given early in the process. This general approval of the planning process idea helps to secure the specific funds that will later be requested. Obviously, the specific needs cannot be known before the research is done and the niches are determined, but seed money should be allocated to get the project moving.

I would suggest that a smaller congregation beginning an effort of this kind allow at least $500 to $1,000 for initial research expenses, and at least

$1,000 to $2,000 for the immediate costs of any printing, promotional expense, or advertising that may initially be recommended. Once the plan is developed and approved, the actual cost of advertising and promotion will probably be many times that amount, depending on what marketing strategies are deemed most helpful. Clearly, for larger congregations, all of the amounts mentioned will need to be larger. A larger congregation will likely be dealing with larger samples or more samples for research, and the advertising expense may be directed at larger markets.

The money designated for research may be used to purchase demographic or psychographic studies, maps, or city-street directories; or to pay focus-group participants or a professional marketing company to conduct the focus groups. If professional services are utilized, the amount budgeted will need to be several times more than the amount indicated above. Typically, a professionally conducted focus group will cost at least $2,500 per group, and seldom is a single focus group session sufficient. Focus groups can be organized and conducted by volunteer church leadership at a much-reduced cost.

3. Create a task force or designate an existing group of congregational leaders to guide the research process. There may be an outreach committee, a strategy planning committee, or some other existing group in the congregation that would logically pursue market-driven planning. If there is not, a special task force may be created for this purpose. Creating a new task force provides the congregation with the opportunity to carefully enlist key people who may not be serving on existing committees. There may be church members with professional expertise who can be enlisted; generally, persons enlisted for a project of this kind should be highly motivated, creative, and progressive. They will be working with the facilitator to explore new and experimental areas of congregational endeavor.

Because the work of market-driven strategy development potentially involves both evangelism and social ministry, it would be desirable to have persons with spiritual gifts and passions in those areas serving on the task force. Vision is another helpful quality for anyone involved in trying to cast and clarify the images of the future for the church. In any congregation, there are some of those right-brain conceptual thinkers who can help the congregation imagine potential futures. As niche possibilities emerge, they will likely indicate other areas of talent and expertise that will need to be involved. Areas of congregational life such as music and education will come into play. As those needs become evident, the task force may be expanded to include the needed expertise.

Once a task force is chosen, the group can develop a schedule for its work. Meeting times and places will be determined, and a general time flow for the process may be projected. Completing these tasks (getting general approval for the effort, securing an initial budget, and selecting a task force) will take the process through the completion of the preparation phase.

Research and Discovery Phase

4. Determine inside research approaches and delegate tasks. The first major work of the task force is to plan the internal research methods that are to be employed. The basic questions the task force should ask and find answers for with regard to research methods are:

A. What are we trying to learn?
B. Through what method can we best learn it?
C. From what persons can we best learn it?
D. What questions do we need to ask?
E. How can we best ask the questions to learn what we need to know? (The reader may note that these questions are similar to those listed in chapter 2 on the subject of the design of research questionnaires.)

Each inside research approach utilized should be expanded and clarified with written answers to these five questions. The completed answers to these five questions in a hypothetical congregation, which we will call Trinity Church, might look like this:

A. What are we trying to learn?
  • Is our church growing or declining numerically?
  • What kinds of people are we most effective in reaching, and where are our current new members coming from geographically, demographically, and sociologically?
B. Through what method can we best learn it?
  • We should study the church records and prepare charts and graphs to show our rate of growth over the past 10 years.

- We need a pin map that shows the residences of all of those who have joined the church in the past five years, and we need to interview a number of the new members to determine their basic lifestyle characteristics and personal values.

C. From what persons can we best learn it?
  - Church records.
  - Those who are newer members of the church.

D. What questions do we need to ask?
  - What brought you to Trinity?
  - What quality of the church most appealed to you when you decided to join?
  - Since you joined, what have you found to be the most appealing aspect of the church?
  - Did you visit other churches when you were deciding where to join? If so, what was the primary factor that led you to join Trinity?

E. How can we best ask the questions to learn what we need to know?
  - We will form two focus groups of newer members with eight to twelve persons in each group.
  - In addition, a written survey will be sent to all of those who joined in the past five years.

This task of recording answers to these key questions helps everyone involved to maintain an awareness of why they are doing the research and what it is designed to accomplish. Once the research methods are set, a schedule of activities can be established to accomplish the tasks. Members of the task force should be delegated to oversee the various elements of the inside research, and the entire task force will develop a time frame by which to have it completed.

Chapter 2 listed some of the research possibilities: church records, maps and graphs created from the records, member questionnaires, focus groups, storytelling sessions, and personal interviews. Several, but not all, of these methods may be selected for use by the task force.

The use of congregational records for inside research is always a part of the process. These records are readily available in most cases, and there is almost no cost involved in compiling and analyzing them. The graphs and maps that will be helpful and informative can be developed by members of the task force or by persons they may enlist. These graphic representations help everyone visualize and better comprehend the meaning of the statistics.

In addition to the church records and maps, at least two of the other four methods should be used. In addition, the task force may think of other ways of seeking inside information.

5. Determine outside research approaches and delegate tasks. The task force will then need to expand its scope of understanding about the congregation and its connection to its community by securing the information that can be gained through outside research. Chapter 4 discussed the choices for outside research as including demographics, psychographics, focus groups, interviews and intercepts, questionnaires, phone surveys, conversations, observations, and high-tech possibilities.

As with inside research, the basic statistical information on the community around the congregation is readily available, and it will almost always be included in the information base. The more sophisticated psychographic data may or may not be available at an affordable price. Among the other research information sources, at least two or three should be used by the task force. The same five questions listed above should be applied.

Task-force members will again be asked to oversee various elements of the outside research, and a time schedule will be established. The entire task force can give general leadership to the process and work together to make major decisions (such as the types of research to be done), but the details of each research effort will be charged to individuals or subgroups. This division of labor provides greater efficiency in the work of the task force. A deadline needs to be established for the completion of all research and the compilation of data so that a time can be set for reporting and analyzing all of it.

Trinity developed the following answers to the five questions as they applied to outside research:

A. What are we trying to learn?
- We want to know which unreached groups in our community our church could effectively reach, and we want to know about groups with unmet needs to which our church should minister.
B. Through what method can we best learn it?
- We will need to secure demographic and lifestyle cluster data for a five-mile radius around the church.

- We will need a separate study of data for the zip code in which the church is located.
- We will need to get clearer demographic information about the typical resident of the community where we are most effectively reaching people. This can be learned by creating a pin map showing the residences of persons who have joined the congregation in the past five years.
- We will need a better understanding of the needs of the people living in the immediate neighborhood of the church. It appears that this information might be best secured by utilizing focus groups and intercept interviews.
- We will also use an observation technique by having members of the church drive the primary highways and streets between the church and where our members live in order to learn from the advertising approaches being used by those selling secular goods and services (for example, billboards and bus shelters). The advertisers have knowledge about marketing to our constituency which we need to learn.

C. From what persons can we best learn it?
- We can best learn from persons randomly selected from the broader community. They will be representative of those we intend to reach.
- The entire population of the area will be analyzed through the use of demographic studies.

D. What questions do we need to ask?
- From the demographics, focus groups, and intercepts, we will ask whether there are specific niche groups with needs our church could address.
- We will ask how our statistics for various groups in our area compare with the national average. In groups where our population is significantly higher than the national average, this may be an indication of a niche we should consider.
- From our observation of billboards of secular advertisers we will ask questions like, "How are secular advertisers appealing to the people who live in our area. What approaches are working for them?"

- With the focus groups and interviews, we want to ask, "What causes you the greatest worry about the future? What concerns do you have about the future of your children and grandchildren? Do you attend a church as often as once a month? Why do you think most people don't go to church? What advice would you give to a church that really wanted to help the community?"

E. How can we best ask the questions to learn what we need to know?
- The questions will need to be phrased carefully and in a way that is not invasive or threatening. We can ask, "Why do you think most people don't go to church?" rather than "Why don't you do go church?" The exception to the impersonal questioning is the one question of, "Do you attend once a month?" This is the best way to identify whether the respondents are actually unchurched. Most people have a religious (denominational) preference and may say they attend church, even if it is only for Christmas or a wedding.

These sample responses illustrate how a planning group might deal with the questions that help clarify the best ways to gather outside research.

6. Hear reports from all research groups. This meeting will be a longer and important one for the task force. They may wish to include some additional congregational leaders in this meeting due to its importance. The individuals and groups who were involved in all of the inside and outside research projects will report. The facilitator and the task force should coordinate the order of those reports and determine the appropriate length of each report. In general, I would suggest that about half of the available meeting time be allocated to reporting, and that the other half be devoted to analysis and interpretation of the reports. I have found that a minimum amount of time for this meeting would involve 90 minutes for the sharing of reports, and 90 minutes for the discussion and analysis of the information.

A more desirable way of scheduling this session would be as an all-day retreat. In many cases, a Saturday will provide the best timing for a retreat. This format will allow the first few hours for reporting from the research groups, and the last few hours for processing and drawing conclusions from the information shared.

When reports are made on the inside research, the task force will be looking for relevant information about what the congregation does well and not so well. A pin map will say some things about geographic areas where the congregation has proven to be effective in outreach. Surveys and other research methods will help to show programmatic or functional areas in which the congregation has been most effective in its work. When outside research reports are given, the task force will be listening for new information and insights about potential niche groups and approaches for future outreach. For example, the demographic data may reveal a large number of people of a certain ethnic or language group living in the vicinity.

7. **Analyze church strengths and potential niche groups.** Ultimately, the outcome of the retreat or reporting session is hoped to be a consensus listing of the strengths of the church and a priority list of potential niche groups. The group should attempt to be objective and honest in the evaluation of strengths. All churches would like to believe that they are friendly and welcoming, but honest observation may bring into question how truly sensitive and caring they are towards outsiders. Before church leaders claim a given strength for the church, they should be sure that their judgment is born out from several sources. In other words, the friendliness is more reliably demonstrated if it emerges from new-member interviews, guest interviews, and church-facility observations (for example, convenient parking, welcoming entrance, or helpful signage), rather than from interviews with long-time members.

Niche Selection Phase

8. **Determine the feasibility and priority of various niches.** Either at the retreat meeting or at a later session, the task force will need to carefully evaluate the potential niches and make some decisions about the order in which to attempt to address them. Chapter 5 provides some guidelines for evaluating market segments. Congregational leaders will need to apply these guidelines to assess how feasible and advisable the segment may be as a focus for outreach or ministry.

9. **Determine the level of passion and calling within the congregation for various niches.** There will be two important questions

to answer in the affirmative before the church begins to work on developing ministry to a given niche group:

A. Is there an inclination for us to adopt this niche group as a potential ministry focus for our congregation?

B. Who in our congregation has a passion or a calling to reach this kind of person? Regardless of how logical and obvious a given niche effort may seem, if either of these questions is answered in the negative, the ministry effort will probably not be effective.

When a niche group surfaces as a possibility, the members of the task force may know of someone in the church with a strong interest or a particular identification with the group. That can be explored through personal conversations with the individual to determine whether there is a calling or a passion for that ministry or outreach. Another way of searching for persons with a particular passion may be to run items in the congregation's publications that ask for persons with certain interests to contact a designated person on the task force. Subsequent conversation will help clarify whether the passion is present.

10. Select niches to be addressed immediately and those to be considered later. Out of all of this consideration, a priority listing of niche efforts will be developed. Some of the niches may be easily addressed, and others may need more time and preparation. The financial cost for some projects may require additional time to secure. The need for ready volunteers may necessitate a delay in the launching of some projects. This priority listing may need to be amended and adjusted over the course of time, but initially it is helpful to have an idea of where the congregation will focus its efforts and energies. A midsize or smaller congregation may want to limit its initial niche outreach efforts to one or two groups; a larger congregation might attempt to focus on three or four to get started.

A task force might decide to begin its practical work with a single niche as an experimental learning effort. I recommend that congregations begin with more than one effort, because experience has shown me that at least one failure is likely, and having multiple lines in the water is more likely to result in a successful ministry launch. If a congregation begins with a single niche and runs into problems, it may scuttle the entire marketing project. Two or more efforts at the beginning increase the probability that one or more will yield positive results.

Strategy Design Phase

11. Design the methods and means by which the niche group will be addressed. One by one the task force will make plans for how the church will conduct the ministry or evangelism to a given niche group. The task is to develop a strategy for addressing the niche. Keep in mind the principle of providing multiple entry points for new persons receiving ministry or outreach efforts. These goals and plans should be committed to writing by the task force or a subgroup of the task force, and if persons who will be directly involved (those with a passion for the work) have been identified, they may be enlisted to help develop the plans.

12. Develop the minimum necessary structure to conduct the ministry. Whatever new ministry or outreach effort is planned will require some degree of organization. The design of the new initiative, however, should not be an occasion to create new and expanded bureaucracies—the simplest and most logical structure will be the best. Minimum organization to create efficient administration and accountability is the goal. Where the congregation has existing structures that can adequately manage the work, new structures may not be required. The particular ministry may only need a coordinator or a small team, with clear understandings of where they go for assistance and guidance. Emerging ministries should not be micromanaged or overmanaged, but neither should they be lone-ranger efforts disconnected from the congregation as a whole. They should be viewed as a part of the total ministry of the congregation.

Marketing Design Phase

13. Apply the earlier research to design the marketing plan for launching the niche project. Chapter 4 includes information about how marketing may be developed to appeal to certain niches. The task force should work on planning the best possible advertising and promotion of the new ministry, working within their budget limits. Chapter 5 also contains helpful suggestions for developing guerilla-marketing approaches that maximize available funds. This offers the congregation the challenge of exercising great creativity to obtain maximum marketing results with minimum investments of limited resources. The task force will need to have a written plan for the progression of marketing efforts.

14. Allocate the resources necessary for the project and its promotion. At the launch of the marketing planning process, some basic budget for the projects was designated. Now, as the plans become more specific, a more precise budget can be requested. The task force will work with the appropriate administrative structures of the church to propose and explain the need for additional resources for doing the ministries and for marketing them. There may be instances in which additional funding is not needed, but most circumstances will require more money than was originally granted.

15. Set a launch date for the project and enlist congregational affirmation, involvement, and prayer support. The individual niche project may only involve a handful of people in the congregation. It may be heavily dependent on one or two individuals with a passion for serving the particular persons who make up the niche. It is important, however, that the entire congregation be aware of the effort and be providing prayer support and any other needed resources, such as volunteers, materials, or promotional assistance. The setting of launch dates will also need to be coordinated with the overall church calendar and other emphases that the church may be doing, and it will need to be done only after the persons directly involved in the effort are on board. A part of the word-of-mouth marketing that is so important to new initiatives will be generated, as members of the congregation become aware of and supportive of the niche effort.

An official launch date for the effort provides the entire congregation with an opportunity to commission or bless the workers who will be involved in the ministry, and it informs everyone of its formal beginning. It also marks the beginning of the marketing strategy that will be employed.

Implementation Phase

16. Begin the work. The task force will empower and encourage the persons conducting the projects and the people leading the marketing of the effort. The new ministries will probably be launched one at a time as the necessary elements are in place. The task force is the oversight group that will coordinate all of the efforts and schedule their beginning.

It is important, however, that the task force coordinate its efforts with other existing leadership groups in the congregation. The primary role of the task force as implementation begins is coordination, not policy making or controlling. This vital coordination with congregational structures, paid staff members, and the larger congregation as a whole will determine the success of the efforts.

17. Adjust the game plan and continue the work. As the various projects begin, there will be unexpected and unintended results. The task force should keep a big-picture concern for them, but each ministry may have its own coordinator or small group of leaders. Either the coordinator of the individual ministry or the task force may see ways in which strategies need to be adjusted and improved. There should be flexibility in the system that allows for constant and quick redirection and improvement. If the plans are not cast in stone by an official congregational vote on every detail, they can be more easily adjusted with emerging circumstances.

Evaluation and Adaptation Phase

18. Secure evaluation of the ministry from those conducting it. Those who lead the ministries will be evaluating the effectiveness of the work as honestly and objectively as they can. The task force will want to establish a regular procedure for having the ministry or outreach workers assess whether the effort is fulfilling its purposes. Such evaluation may be done by a combination of written surveys, interviews, or observations.

19. Secure evaluation from those who have been recipients. A second form of evaluation is for the task force to secure evaluation from those who are the recipients or the intended recipients of the ministry or outreach. These are the persons who can provide the best insight into whether it is working and why it is or is not fulfilling its mission. Evaluation from these persons may be obtained by personal interviews by ministry leadership or by carefully worded written surveys.

20. Compile the lessons learned. Every experimental ministry effort has lessons to teach us. In this sense, no experiment in ministry is a failure. If the effort completely fails to fulfill its purpose to reach the people it had hoped to reach, it still provides leaders with valuable information about what works and does not work. The analysis of the failures becomes important, because it is in this process that the priceless insights for future efforts come to us.

The market planning task force will compile, discuss, and record all of these lessons, including the evaluations that were done in steps 18 and 19. These lessons learned will not only be helpful for congregational efforts in the future, but these school-of-hard-knocks lessons may be helpful to others attempting similar strategies in other places. This is how our local experiments may enhance the overall effectiveness of the larger mission of God.

21. Make a determination of whether to continue, how to adapt, or how to otherwise apply the learnings of the experience. The task force, along with the ministry leaders, will at some point decide whether the ministry should continue, be changed, or be discontinued. Reasons for pulling the plug on an effort might be:

A. The ministry is not working—the intended niche is not being reached.
B. The people who are leading the ministry do not have the necessary passion, skills, or commitment to make it work.
C. The congregation is not supportive or interested in the effort.
D. The marketing costs are too great for the benefits they produce in terms of ministry or outreach accomplished. It must be kept in mind that depending on the purpose of the ministry, no visible benefits may be expected for some.
E. The niche is responding, but in numbers too small as to have significant results or to justify the resources and efforts being invested. An example might be a project to help middle-aged single adults find social relationships. If those responding from the potential niche group were only a few persons in the community, and if the cost of newspaper advertising to reach them were substantial, it might be determined that the results being obtained did not justify the cost incurred.

When a market-driven project is laid to rest, there is a great tendency to put it quietly out of its misery and to feel a sense of failure. On the contrary, a failed effort should be celebrated, and its benefits should be highlighted. The effort probably did some good for someone, either the ministry participant or ministry recipient. The effort resulted in important lessons being learned. The effort itself is a sign of life and entrepreneurial energy in the church. All of these and other outcomes can be legitimately celebrated. The celebration might take the form of a time in a worship service when the above results would be acknowledged, or a recognition of those persons who had worked in the effort. Congregations do not often do a good job of celebrating their successes, not to mention their poor habits of celebrating failures. This occasion becomes an opportunity to recognize the work people have done, the sincerity of the efforts that were expended, the value of the lessons learned, and the accomplishments of the project— even if they were meager.

If the ministry or outreach is succeeding, it may be continued and enhanced. There will still be lessons to be learned and recorded. The successful effort may also lead to other possibilities for new niches or new ways to reach people with innovative techniques. Small successes can be the building blocks for more and greater successes.

Much of the success of niche marketing efforts will be determined by the attitude and outlook of the congregation. If those who are members see the congregation as being a community-oriented, beyond-the-walls effort, their niche projects will more likely have the needed motivation and passion to succeed.

7

Your Congregation
Restaurant or Home-Delivered Meals?

For too long, congregations have suffered from an edifice complex. We have built and furnished our buildings with a naïve hope that if we built them, the people would come. Several years ago, the movie *Field of Dreams* reminded us of the romance of believing that our fondest dreams can come true. An Iowa farmer who was an avid baseball fan became convinced that if he turned a cornfield into a fully equipped ballpark, the people would come to watch the games. Unfortunately, the fulfillment of the fantasy portrayed in the movie does not often happen in the real world. After many years of hoping fine facilities would automatically draw people to our houses of worship, we are reluctantly recognizing that society has changed. The world has morphed to a point where it is becoming clear that no matter where or how well you build it, they may not come. Congregations must find ways to move beyond their walls. There are biblical mandates that make this clear, and the practical realities of our age underline it. The good news of God's redemptive message, and the cup of cold water offered in service to others, must be taken to people where they live.

The relevant congregation of this day sees itself as a home-delivered meals operation rather than a restaurant. The congregation's physical facility may provide the central planning and preparation station from which you move out in ministry, but the services you offer the world have to be delivered. The meals you deliver must be prepared according to the needs and interests of the people you serve before you deliver them. Those who are involved in the delivery must see themselves as servants. First of all, they are servants of God; second, they are servants of those to whom they deliver the food they have to offer. The "food" delivered by "home-delivered meals" congregations may be conferences and training opportunities on subjects of vital concern to people. The "food" offered by the congregation may be counseling services, spiritual guidance, or a host of other needed services or resources.

The entire effort described in this book is an application of marketing principles to congregational outreach and ministry. I believe that there are many valuable principles from secular marketing disciplines that can be transferred to church use. As these chapters have demonstrated, however, there is one overwhelming difference between the corporate marketing environment and the context of the faith community: God.

The subject of our marketing in the context of the faith community is the God who is revealed in the Scriptures. The congregation seeks to make known God's existence, goodness, and personal love for humankind. The motivation for the marketing efforts is God. Believers are compelled, "constrained," as Paul writes (2 Cor. 5:14), by God's love to share this good news with the world. The methodology of the marketing is influenced by God and by the ethical ideals revealed in God's Word. This means that manipulative or coercive methods are not used. Congregations will be careful to not over promise in their marketing, and to not practice bait-and-switch advertising. (Bait and switch is the unscrupulous advertising practice of offering a special deal on a product, but when the customer arrives to buy it, the product is not available and the vendor attempts to sell one that is not such a good deal.) The marketing methods employed by healthy congregations are above reproach ethically.

The strategy of the marketing, if it is to be successful, depends on God. Any of these plans, separated from God's constant guidance and correction, will amount to nothing of spiritual significance. Resources to support the marketing depend on God's provision. Most congregations do not have sufficient funds to buy network affiliate television time or full-page ads in major newspapers. That means they must tap into the immeasurable riches of God to find the money, time, energy, and creativity to reach the world with their life-giving message. This enters into the mystical and unexplainable realm of life where we experience seeming coincidences and sudden strokes of luck which can be understood as God at work to provide for that which pleases God.

A Simple, Clear Sense of Purpose

As I was researching and outlining the material for this book, I had the opportunity to spend time with Dr. Ken Blanchard. Blanchard is the author of many best-selling books on corporate management and leadership development, including *The One-Minute Manager*. He is the cofounder of FaithWalk, a national effort to enhance the spirituality and Christian leadership of the laity in churches. FaithWalk is a marketplace ministry designed to maximize the influence of business and community leaders. Blanchard and his cofounder, Phil Hodges, lead FaithWalk leadership seminars in cities across the country.

I spoke with Blanchard about my plans for this book. He affirmed the idea of applying sound marketing approaches to congregational outreach strategies. He also urged me to emphasize the spiritual aspect of congregational health and growth. Blanchard shared an experience he had in his home church.

He said that a new pastor came to the church a few years earlier. The congregation had engaged in strategic planning through the years, and documents that laid out the church's plans for the future were already in place. Some of the material, however, was rather academic and complex. The new pastor came with a desire to simplify and clarify the vision of the church. He suggested that the congregation summarize all of its intentions for the future by simply proclaiming, "We are committed to doing things that will cause Jesus to smile."

Blanchard said that the outcome of this simple, new spiritual focus for the church was phenomenal. Everyone in the congregation was able to understand and remember the idea that "we are here as a church to do things that make Jesus smile." This put all of the congregation's ministries in the context of a heartfelt desire to please Christ. The church became healthier, and it began to see a level of growth beyond any it had experienced previously.

Simply refocusing a congregation's ministry as service to God and others is a good example of how the spiritual element is essential to all congregational planning and coordination. A spiritual emphasis in the market-driven planning process outlined in chapter 6 was considered. Because of the nature of spirituality and its impact on planning, however, congregations involved in this process must ensure that a spiritual focus permeates every step of the process from beginning to end.

The spiritual leaders of a congregation can do a great deal to involve the entire congregation in a spiritual process that supports, informs, and inspires the market-planning effort. I would suggest an ongoing journey of spirituality in the planning process that would include prayer, pulpit reinforcement, and personal reflection.

Prayer

Prayer is essential to any congregational planning. What we hope to develop in a congregation plan is not our best guess at what might work; rather, a plan for a faith community is, at best, our clearest understanding of the purposes of God for this congregation. The larger context of planning is to gain insight into where God has been in the history of this congregation, where God is in its present, and where God wills the congregation to go in the future. This kind of planning requires the best of our creative thinking and analysis, and it requires constant listening to the leadership of God's Spirit through prayer. God can lead through our thoughts and prayers; God can lead through the inspiration and wisdom of the Scriptures; God can lead through the expertise of those from whom we seek counsel; and God can lead through the mysterious, inner witness of the voice we hear with spiritual ears.

Prayer can be exercised in the decision to engage in a market-driven planning process, and it should be a part of the selection of the persons who will make up the planning task force. At every step in the process, prayer is a vital element. The task force will wish to include times for corporate prayer in their meetings. The congregation as a whole is thus made aware of the planning process and encouraged to intercede for its effectiveness. When potential niche groups for future ministry are considered, the task force will pray for leadership from God with regard to where to begin. These niches represent precious persons whom God loves. Decisions about how the congregation should respond to those persons and their needs can only be made with spiritual legitimacy when much prayer is included in the process.

The persons who are enlisted to engage in niche ministries should also be encouraged to pray about their involvement. We hope that such volunteers would be in place because of special giftedness, a sense of calling, and a driving passion for the work to which they put their hands. When all of this is true, it will be a natural and necessary thing for those leaders to pray for the people to whom they will minister.

Pulpit Reinforcement

The spiritual nature of niche ministry can be taught from the pulpit. There are many times in the life of a congregation when relevant, effective preaching can be done to inform, challenge, and inspire the congregation to participate in specific ministry projects.

After a congregation has engaged in a process of discovering its core values and determining its basic strengths, a preacher may prepare a series of sermons, with one sermon on each of the core values or key strengths of the congregation. (*The Manual for Values-based Tactical Planning* cited in this book's bibliography has helpful resources for discovering congregational values.) This is an opportunity to remind the people of what they value, show them if and how that value is biblical and relevant to their faith, and inspire them to live out the value in acts of service. The market-driven planning process outlined in this book focuses on congregational strengths more than values, but both are important. The values are the inner passions that motivate and direct individuals and groups. Congregational strengths are the unique points of special giftedness or resources that provide a congregation with opportunities to excel.

As the congregation begins to focus on specific niche groups and their needs, there will be opportunity to preach a sermon or a series of sermons that highlight the people who make up those niches. Biblical stories help to highlight the needs of such people or examples of how God's servants related to them. Preaching can be a way to sensitize the congregation to daily opportunities to touch lives redemptively through service. The sermon also provides the occasion for God to speak to additional people about getting involved and for them to respond to God's call to participate in the ministry project.

Some of the material in the introduction to this book was, in fact, prepared originally as a series of sermons. I was attempting to sensitize a congregation to the ministry opportunities around them, and help them see Jesus as a model of effective, personalized care. The Bible contains stories, parables, and teachings to illustrate almost every conceivable life situation and ministry challenge. Careful exegesis and application of biblical thought can provide a part of the spiritual foundation for engaging in people-sensitive ministries.

The pulpit and preaching, however, are not the only way to give emphasis to the spirituality of serving human need. The congregation, through various kinds of studies, seminars, and training classes is able to call and equip persons for active involvement in service to others through niche projects initiated in market-driven planning.

Personal Reflection

Members of the staff and the planning task force should be urged to spend time in reflection and meditation throughout the market-driven planning process. In addition to the prayer disciplines mentioned earlier, there is value in silent meditation and theological reflection. It is often in these times of quiet solitude that God speaks with new insights and creative ideas. When the task force meets, it can be a time of bringing together all of the products of individual listening that task-force members have heard as they have listened.

The facilitator of the planning process may wish to ask frequently, "What has God been saying to you about what we discussed in our last meeting?" Out of the spiritual seeking of God's people, engaged individually and collectively in a search for God's guidance, wonderful new approaches to ministry can come.

Keeping a constant awareness of the spiritual nature of the market-driven planning in minds of participants, congregations can utilize the best of marketing principles and achieve new and exciting levels of ministry and outreach. There is hope for God's church in this world. There is hope for smaller and midsize congregations if they are willing to adapt to the new challenges and opportunities of the new cultural setting in which they live. Congregations that will narrow and focus their efforts, address the needs of niches, and change to reach specific people groups have good reason for optimism.

The greatest cause for maintaining hope, however, is not the excellent use of secular approaches; it is the fact that the people of God represent God's chosen way to redeem humanity. God will not neglect or abandon communities of faith as they pursue the mission given to them by God's own design.

There are many images that have been used to describe this new way of looking at congregational enterprise. Many congregations speak of getting beyond the walls; others emphasize taking it to the streets. The metaphor of home-delivered meals that began this chapter is just one other way of describing a congregation that sees the needs in the community and mobilizes itself to proactively go to where the needs exist and where the opportunities for outreach are richest.

As we move further into the 21st century, I hope that many congregations will find their niche or niches, and that this clarity of mission will lead to greater effectiveness. I hope this for God's sake and for the sake of the survival of communities of faith. Most of all, I maintain this hope for the sake of the individual lives that will be touched and changed because God's people cared.

NOTES

Chapter 1

1. George Barna, *The Second Coming of the Church* (Nashville: Word Publishing Co., 1998), 43–44.

2. Mike Regele, *Death of the Church* (Grand Rapids, Mich.: Zondervan Publishing House, 1995), 20.

3. Robert Dale, *Leadership for a Changing Church* (Nashville: Abingdon Press, 1998), 27–28.

4. Lyle Schaller, "Responding to the Competition," *Net Results* 20, no. 12 (December 1999): 11–12.

5. George Barna, *The Second Coming of the Church*, 44–46.

Chapter 2

1. Barna, *The Second Coming of the Church*, 203–204.

2. Alexander Hiam and Charles Schewe, *The Portable MBA in Marketing* (New York: Wiley & Sons, 1992), 129–32.

3. Bob Perry, Ray Spears, and Stephen Welch, *Manual for Values-based Tactical Planning* (Richmond, Va.: O.H.A., 1991). Available from Organizational Health Associates, 309 Burnwick Road, Richmond, VA 23227. Web site: organizationalhealth.org; cost: $24.95 plus postage and handling.

4. Tom Steffen, "Congregational Character: From Stories to Story," *Journal of the American Society for Church Growth* 11 (winter 2000): 26.

Chapter 3

1. Rick Warren, *The Purpose Driven Church* (Grand Rapids, Mich.: Zondervan Publishing House, 1995), 173.

2. Ibid., 158.

3. Al Ries, *Positioning: The Battle for Your Mind* (New York: McGraw-Hill, 1981), 46.

4. Peter Drucker, *Managing for Results* (New York: Harper & Row, 1987), 93.

5. Peter Drucker, *Innovation and Entrepreneurship: Practice and Principles* (New York: Harper & Row, 1987), 120.

Chapter 4

1. John Berrigan and Carl Finkbeiner, *Segmentation Marketing: New Methods for Capturing Business Markets* (New York: HarperCollins, 1992), 28.

2. William Young Jr., "Leading the Hatcher Memorial Baptist Church of Richmond, Virginia in Intentional Evangelism" (Ph.D. diss., The Southern Baptist Theological Seminary, 1998), 122.

3. Sarah White, *The Complete Idiot's Guide to Marketing Basics* (New York: Simon & Schuster, 1997), 68.

4. Warren, *The Purpose Driven Church*, 190–91.

Chapter 5

1. White, *The Complete Idiot's Guide to Marketing Basics*, 9.

2. Ibid., 176.

3. Ibid., 176.

4. Hiam and Schewe, *The Portable MBA in Marketing*, 203.

5. Jennifer Lawton, "The Two Faces of Niche Marketing," <www.entreworld.org> (2001).

6. Pat Means, "Prospering in a Niche Market," <www.entreworld.org> (2001).

7. Arlyn Tobias Gajilan, "Wish I'd Thought of That" in *Fortune Small Business* 11, no. 3 (2001): 1.

8. Gifford Pinchot III, *Intrapreneuring: Why You Don't Have to Leave the Corporation to Become an Entrepreneur* (New York: Harper & Row, 1985), 89.

9. Regis McKenna, *The Regis Touch: Million-Dollar Advice from America's Top Marketing Consultant* (Hartford, Conn.: Addison-Wesley Publishing, 1985), 3.

10. Rosabeth Moss Kanter, *The Change Masters* (New York: Simon and Schuster, 1983), 121.

11. Jay Conrad Levinson, *Guerilla Marketing: Secrets for Making Big Profits from Your Small Business* (New York: Houghton Mifflin, 1993), 7.

12. Hiam and Schewe, *The Portable MBA in Marketing*, 229–30.

13. White, *The Complete Idiot's Guide to Marketing*, 109.

14. Ibid., 160–63.

15. Berrigan and Finkbeiner, *Segmentation Marketing*, 151.

16. William E. Rothschild, *How to Gain (and Maintain) the Competitive Advantage in Business* (New York: McGraw-Hill Book Co., 1984), 117.

17. Bernd Schmitt and Alex Siminson, *Marketing Aesthetics: The Strategic Management of Brands, Identity and Image* (New York: Simon and Schuster, 1997), 59, 167.

BIBLIOGRAPHY

Albert, Kenneth J. *The Strategic Management Handbook*. New York: McGraw-Hill, 1983.

Barker, John. *Strategic Thinking*. Scottsdale, Ariz.: Barker & Associates, 1999.

Barna, George. *Maximizing Your Ministry Impact: Serving Effectively in a Changing Culture*. Glendale, Calif.: Barna Research Group, 1995.

———. *The Second Coming of the Church*. Nashville: Word Publishing, 1998.

Berrigan, John, and Carl Finkbeiner. *Segmentation Marketing: New Methods for Capturing Business Markets*. New York: Harper-Collins, 1992.

Blanchard, Ken. Conversation with author, Williamsburg, Va., May 8, 2001.

Britt, Stewart Henderson. *Psychological Principles of Marketing and Consumer Behavior*. Lexington, Mass.: D. C. Heath and Co., 1978.

Cupit, Tony. *Biblical Models for Evangelism: 1st Century Strategies for the 21st Century Church*. Falls Church, Va.: Baptist World Alliance, 1997.

Dale, Robert D. *Leadership for a Changing Church: Charting the Shape of the River*. Nashville: Abingdon Press, 1998.

———. *Leading Edge: Leadership Strategies from the New Testament*. Nashville: Abingdon Press, 1996.

Drucker, Peter. *Innovation and Entrepreneurship: Practice and Principles*. New York: Harper & Row, 1987.

———. *Managing for Results: Economic Tasks and Risk-Taking Decisions*, rev ed. New York: HarperBusiness, 1993.

Gajilan, Arlyn Tobias. "Wish I'd Thought of That," *Fortune Small Business* 11, no. 3 (2001).

Gilder, George. *The Spirit of Enterprise*. New York: Simon and Schuster, 1984.

Hiam, Alexander, and Charles D. Schewe. *The Portable MBA in Marketing*. New York: Wiley and Sons, Inc., 1992.

Hulbert, James M. *Marketing: A Strategic Perspective*. New York: Impact Publishing Co., 1986.

Kanter, Rosabeth Moss. *The Change Masters*. New York: Simon and Schuster, 1983.

Lawton, Jennifer. "The Two Faces of Niche Marketing," <www.entreworld.org>, 2001.

Levinson, Jay Conrad. *Guerilla Marketing: Secrets for Making Big Profits from Your Small Business*. New York: Houghton Mifflin, 1993.

Marino, Kenneth E. *Forecasting Sales and Planning Profits*. Chicago: Probus Publishing Co., 1986.

McKenna, Regis. *The Regis Touch: Million-Dollar Advice from America's Top Marketing Consultant*. Hartford, Conn.: Addison-Wesley Publishing, 1985.

McQuarrie, Edward F. *The Market Research Toolbox*. Thousand Oaks, Calif.: Sage Publications, Inc., 1996.

Means, Pat. "Prospering in a Niche Market," <www.entreworld.org>, 2001.

Miller, William C. *The Creative Edge*. Reading, Mass.: Addison-Wesley Publishing Co., 1987.

Perry, Robert L. *Pass the Power, Please!* Richmond, Va.: Organizational Health Associates, 1995.

Perry, Robert L., Ray Spears, and Stephen Welch. *Manual for Values-based Tactical Planning*. Richmond, Va.: Organizational Health Associates, 1991.

Pinchot, Gifford, III. *Intrapreneuring: Why You Don't Have to Leave the Corporation to Become an Entrepreneur*. New York: Harper & Row, 1985.

Regele, Mike. *Death of the Church*. Grand Rapids, Mich.: Zondervan Publishing House, 1995.

Ries, Al. *Positioning: The Battle for Your Mind*. New York: McGraw-Hill, 1981.

Rothschild, William E. *How to Gain (and Maintain) the Competitive Advantage in Business*. New York: McGraw-Hill, 1984.

Schaller, Lyle E. "Responding to the Competition," *Net Results* 20, no. 12 (December 1999).

Schmitt, Bernd, and Siminson, Alex. *Marketing Aesthetics: The Strategic Management of Brands, Identity Image*. New York: Simon & Schuster, 1997.

Steffen, Tom. "Congregational Character: From Stories to Story," *Journal of the American Society for Church Growth* 11 (winter 2000).

Warren, Rick. *The Purpose Driven Church*. Grand Rapids, Mich.: Zondervan Publishing House, 1995.

White, Sarah. *The Complete Idiot's Guide to Marketing Basics*. New York: Simon & Schuster, 1997.

Young, William, Jr. "Leading the Hatcher Memorial Baptist Church of Richmond, Virginia, in Intentional Evangelism." Doctoral diss., Southern Baptist Theological Seminary, Louisville, Ky., 1998.